COMMENDATIONS

'If you are looking for a biblical, balanced, and proven example of what it means to be a purpose-driven church in a British context, the answer is in your hand. David Beer is a visionary pastor who is modelling for all of us what it means to take the Great Commandment and Great Commission seriously. I highly recommend this book. Read it. Study it. Practise it!'

Rick Warren, author of *The Purpose Driven Church*

'I have known David Beer for more than a quarter of a century. He has been my mentor, my colleague and my friend. And if I know anything about David I know this – he is passionate about what makes local churches grow.

David has spent the last 40 years thinking, praying, studying, debating, researching, writing and teaching about church growth. But far more impressively, he has spent each one of them growing churches. Every church that David has led has grown – and grown dramatically. It's this combination of understanding and delivery that makes this book different.'

Steve Chalke – Founder, Oasis Trust and Faithworks

'The fact that we have so many churches and church leaders with an appetite for growth is great news for the Kingdom. It's even greater news that we have informed practitioners who are equipped to enable that growth to take place. David Beer is one such enabler.

David's experience and expertise has been a vital contribution to our work at the Evangelical Alliance as we have sought to challenge and equip our churches to establish good models of disciple-making churches with purpose.

Releasing Your Church to Grow is a hands-on resource which will take the reader from the process of vision-casting to its practical application.'

Joel Edwards
General Director, Evangelical Alliance

This book is dedicated to the pastors and leaders
who have served with me at Frinton Free Church

Releasing Your Church to Grow

DAVID BEER

KINGSWAY PUBLICATIONS
EASTBOURNE

Unless otherwise indicated, biblical quotations are
from the New International Version © 1973, 1978, 1984
by the International Bible Society.
NLT = New Living Translation copyright © 1996 by
Tyndale Charitable Trust. Used by permission of Tyndale
House Publishers, Wheaton, Illinois, USA.

ISBN 1 84291 140 6

Published by
KINGSWAY COMMUNICATIONS LTD
Lottbridge Drove, Eastbourne BN23 6NT, England.
Email: books@kingsway.co.uk

Book design and production for the publishers by
Bookprint Creative Services, P.O. Box 827, BN21 3YJ, England.
Printed in Great Britain.

Contents

Thanks

Sometimes God puts people in your life in such a way that you know it is God who has arranged it. It is what is often referred to as a 'divine appointment'. We all have them. There have been many throughout my life, but in recent years two in particular: Rick Warren, Pastor of Saddleback Church, Orange County, California, who loves pastors and has committed his life to assisting and encouraging them, and Dan Southerland, who devotes his energies to helping pastors bring positive changes to their own lives and to the churches that they pastor. Both men have been a personal inspiration and example to me. Both have challenged me to think again about what it means to build a healthy church and to help other pastors do the same. I am greatly indebted to them for their input into this book.

My thanks also to the pastors and church leaders I have had the privilege of serving with during the years of my ministry.

Thanks to my family: Dorothy; Leisa, our daughter, now a pastor's wife and married to Steve; their children and our precious grandchildren, Brianna and Jackson; our son Keith, now married to Faith.

I would also like to thank Richard Herkes, Publishing

Director of Kingsway Publications, and Carolyn Owen, Editorial Co-ordinator, for their patience, ideas and encouragement.

David Beer

Foreword

There is little room for doubt about God's intention for his church. When Jesus declared 'I will build my church' he made it obvious. God's plan is for the church to grow, to have influence, to be healthy, to be powerful. Jesus intends to build his church. You have to get a church really sick to keep Jesus from being able to build and bless it!

And yet that is exactly what we have done! One recent study indicates that in the UK and the US today, 85 per cent of churches are in decline. What a sad statement! It also found that 14 per cent of churches are growing by transfers from other churches – which is not the way we want to grow. But the most amazing finding was that less than one per cent of churches are growing by conversion growth – by seeing people come to faith in Christ! If God's plan is to grow his church, how do we get in on that plan? How do we see what God is doing in the world and join him in it? How do we release our churches to grow?

This book by my friend David Beer deals with that issue squarely. I am delighted to recommend David to you for three reasons. First, he has personally led a church through renewal and significant growth. He is not a theoretician; he is a practitioner! Second, David is a student of church growth and church

11

health. He has spent his life studying what is going on around the world in God's church. Third, David is leading a movement of churches called the Purpose Driven Churches of the United Kingdom. This group of hundreds of churches from all denominations is totally committed to discovering and doing the purposes of God – and God is indeed working among them! When Rick Warren and his team at Saddleback chose David to lead this movement in the UK, they made a wise choice!

But beyond David's qualifications, the book is a good one! David deals with the key issues related to growth and change in the church. From purpose to preparation, from structure to small groups, David covers the basics. This book takes the complicated challenge of getting a church healthy and focused, and breaks it down into simple bite-size pieces. The best thing about this book is that it is do-able by the average pastor! David has written real truths about the real issues of church growth.

If you only read one church growth book this year, make it this one!

Dan Southerland
Director of Church Transitions Inc.
and author of *Transitioning: Leading Your Church
Through Change*

Introduction

Throughout my ministry, I have always tried to get God's vision for the local church. For example, in June 1987, I wrote an article for our church magazine under the title 'Our Vision for the Future', giving the following five goals:

- to proclaim the gospel;
- to be a fellowship in which people can find God's love and forgiveness;
- to be a fellowship in which every member can be encouraged to grow;
- to be a fellowship which serves the community;
- to be a church that is a support base for mission and wider ministry.

I added: 'We know from the Bible that God wants us to be this kind of church.'

This was long before I had read Rick Warren's book *The Purpose Driven Church*, or even before that book was written. So when I did read it, some ten years later, I quickly identified with the five biblical purposes he describes from Matthew 22:37–40 and 28:19–20. Rick calls these two statements the Great Commandment and the Great Commission. The same five biblical purposes can be found in Acts 2:42–47, a section of Scripture described by some as what a fully functioning biblical community looks like.

In my church magazine I went on to say that we meet together each week:

- to *celebrate* the life of God;
- to *cultivate* personal growth in Christ;
- to *care* about one another;
- to *communicate* Christ to the world.

'This is the glue that holds us together,' I wrote. 'This is what our church is all about, and every member has a place and part to play in all this.'

Since writing the article, I have tried to develop these principles. Looking back, I can see the gaps in what I was trying to say. In recent years, I have tried to fill those gaps and more adequately articulate the principles I have always held dear to my heart about what a healthy, growing church should be. I know I am not alone in this. There are many leaders who hold deeply the same convictions about church, but have needed a framework to implement them. That is what this book is all about.

Note: Some of the material for this book also appears in my earlier publication, *50 Ways to Help Your Church Grow* (Kingsway Publications, 2000).

1

Churches Come in All Shapes and Sizes

We can no longer expect people to turn up at church buildings on Sundays. But one thing is for certain: if we *don't* expect them, they won't turn up! So often local churches get what they expect. Lack of expectation is not a sign of health. Before anything can happen in terms of outreach, someone in the church must have a faith-motivated dream.

It is frequently said, 'We should go out to serve and support the community rather than always expect people to come to us.' This is true, as long as we do not completely abandon the expectation of people coming to church. If we do, our churches will become ill prepared to welcome new people, especially unchurched people, and the result will be Christian huddles. Remember that if your mission in the community is successful, sooner or later new people are going to want to come and join your church. Why can't we serve in the community *and* expect people to come and join us? Why can't we do both? Why can't we achieve that balance?

Too many churches fall into the trap of thinking that there is only one way to be the church. Around the world there are multitudes of examples and plenty of dreams about being the church. Indeed there are so many that some leaders and members of the congregation can find it almost overwhelming.

But we shouldn't give up. If 'business as usual' is not working, we must find another way, even though there will be resistance. The following letter to a local newspaper is a typical attitude toward Church of England churches that try to change:

> Although I no longer attend church, I have supported the parish church over a good number of years. My immediate family have all attended and participated in services at All Saints' Church and are still regular churchgoers. I found reading the front-page article [of the newspaper] regarding the proposed plans to alter the church very disturbing.
>
> I was born here and my sister and I were christened in the church, as were my children. My grandparents' funeral services were held in this church, as mine may well be.
>
> The vicar wants to remove the, as he puts it, old choir stalls because there is no longer a choir. As I understand it, the choristers were moved down into the transept at his behest. The vicar might only be here for a few more years, so what guarantee that the next vicar will not want to have a traditional choir and to make more use of the fine organ?
>
> As for car parking, there are three car parks within easy reach of the church and another one in this position can only cause access problems.
>
> Today's attitude of 'change for change's sake' must stop at some stage.

There are many Church of England ministers who have faced almost identical sentiments. While trying to respect the writer's point of view, church leaders recognise that change is necessary, not 'change for change's sake', but in order to connect with the culture without compromising the Christian message. The balance between compromise and irrelevance is one of the major issues to be grasped by the church.

There is plenty of dreaming going on. Time and again we read articles and hear seminars encouraging different ways of being the church: 'We need to be churches without walls'; 'We have to take the good news out into the world'; 'We need to step out into the community, instead of expecting the community to come to us'. We are told to 'face up to reality' and 'be prepared to pay the price of mission'; 'we need to take risks'; 'it's time for a new missionary zeal'; 'the churches need to step out of their comfort zone'. We may applaud such statements and feel motivated by the inspiration of the speakers and writers, but in a sense it's all been heard before, and the really big issue for many congregations and leaders is, 'Yes, but how?'

'We need a new confidence in taking the good news out of the confines of the church and into the world!' Yes, but how?

'This is the time for social care initiatives and partnering with local authorities!' Yes, but how?

'It's time for radical church planting!' Yes, but how?

'It's time to change attitudes and buildings and practices in order to reach people for Christ!' Yes, but how?

'The church must be serious about mission!' Yes, but how?

There are plenty of dreams. There are plenty of challenges to face. There are multitudes of church models to excite us. But what so many congregations and their leaders need is a process for leading change in their own local church. They need a road map.

Examples and models of being church can make us think differently and broaden our horizons, but they are not good road maps. They do not always answer the question 'Yes, but how?', but they do show what can be done. They provide inspiration. There is much to be learned from them in terms of principles. Such models can be an encouragement to other churches, not by copying the methods, though some ideas are worth copying, but by learning from the principles on which they build.

Many models of church

There are more churches and more Christians today than in any previous generation. There are literally thousands of different ways in which churches are fulfilling the Great Commission (Matthew 28:19) and making disciples. There are so many patterns and models of being church. In the UK alone, even against the background of an overall decline in church attendance, there are exciting and innovative examples of new or changing churches in all kinds of social and cultural settings.

Some principles are easily identified with one particular church. For example, there is the 'seeker' principle pioneered by the Willow Creek Community Church in South Barrington, Illinois. Then there is the principle of being motivated by purpose, in contrast to being driven by buildings, finance, personality, tradition or other factors: the purpose-driven church identified with the Saddleback Community Church, Orange County, California. There are other models of being church which have captured international interest, such as the cell church – a church that meets primarily in small groups in homes, workplaces, schools and colleges – and natural church development, which describes principles for church health put forward by Christian Schwarz, head of the Institute for Church Development in Germany. These particular examples of church have caught the imagination of many church leaders.

Lesser-known ways of working have been developed by mainstream Christian denominations or groups of churches working together. There is a lot of creative thinking going on. The number of new shapes and forms of church emerging at the beginning of the twenty-first century is encouraging. Anglican clergyman Michael Moynagh says, 'These experiments could herald a dramatic shift in evangelistic strategy – one that builds new expressions of church for a new era.'[1] Let's look at some of these new expressions in more detail. What follows is simply observation. No attempt has been made at

---

[1] Michael Moynagh, *Changing World, Changing Church* (Monarch Books, 2001), p. 15.

this point to evaluate and say what can, or cannot, be learned. But as Joel Edwards, General Director of the Evangelical Alliance, said, 'How might we work together to reach the UK for Christ? It can be done, with a little imagination.'[2]

The seeker church

The Willow Creek Community Church focuses on reaching and serving those outside the church. This seeker model has influenced countless churches worldwide and brought fresh thinking about who the church is for. It has sharpened awareness of the gap between churchgoer and non-churchgoer, and it has reawakened a desire to reach those who would never normally darken the door of a local church. Local churches recognise the importance of Willow Creek's commitment to cultural relevance and genuine pastoral care of the community. The Willow Creek church has inspired a variety of initiatives, many of them focused not so much on changing worship, but on connecting with the community and building relationships.

Café-style churches have been one attempt to connect with the community. A room or even the worship area of a church building is arranged so that people can sit at tables with refreshments while interactive worship and teaching takes place. There are pub churches too. An old and vandalised pub in Plymouth was made into a place where Christians worship and to which unchurched people are invited. Adrian Hancock, writing about The Crown in the 1998 Spring issue of *Church Growth Digest*, says: 'Attracting adults and making them feel comfortable on their own terms is important if they are ever to join the church and become worshippers, or even listen with an open mind to the Christian message.' As with other pub churches, such as Holy Joe's in London and Zac's Place in Swansea, the seeker influence is evident. One church tripled the number of people attending their normal worship service in

2 Joel Edwards, *Idea*, March/April 2003, p. 3.

just two successive evenings by meeting in a Starbucks coffee shop.

Worship is no longer necessarily a Sunday event either. As work patterns change, so midweek worship is increasing, and this can take place in the daytime as well as evenings. Worship is not confined to the sanctuary of a church and now takes place among Christians in their workplace.

People who have attended Alpha, or a similar seeker course, have sometimes remained together to form what might be referred to as an Alpha church. Alpha churches meet on Sundays or weekdays.

These churches are examples of creative initiatives, which may or may not have been inspired by other churches. The department for Research and Training in Mission of the Baptist Union of Great Britain is engaged in a research project called 'Emerging Church', which looks for initiatives that point to or embody new expressions of church. These include:

- Enigma in Milton Keynes – an ecumenical project using a café church;
- Church Without Walls – an Anglican bar-based church in Birmingham;
- NGM-Eden, which meets in various venues in the UK and targets youth and the club culture;
- Sacred Three in Cambridge – an Anglican initiative featuring alternative worship ideas within the liturgical arena that meets monthly;
- The Sanctuary in Bath, which meets in an Anglican church and offers monthly alternative worship and discussion-based small groups.

The emphasis for so many of these churches is on reaching people where they are and identifying needs within the community and trying to meet those needs. Some churches develop specialist ministries. There are churches that provide respite care to families with disabled children, and there are those that reach out to families whose children are in trouble with teenage gangs.

Darrell Jackson, Mission Adviser at the Baptist Union, says,

There has to be a variety of models of church. Some of these will look like existing churches, and some will be totally different and will meet in a pub lounge on a Wednesday night. Some will draw upon ancient liturgical traditions as much as contemporary music. The thing that works best is being creative, giving people an opportunity to encounter God and being authentic. But, in every case, the churches that have seen an increase in membership or attendance are those that have their focus on reaching out to their local community.[3]

The seeker movement has motivated some churches to target particular age or cultural groups. Although many church leaders in Britain dislike the idea of targeting, often associated with US churches, there are probably as many as 100 youth churches or congregations in the UK. One of the best known is Soul Survivor, which is a network of UK churches. Although targeting may be unpopular, it has proved effective in reaching people in their own cultural and social environment. It is only after people have become mature believers that we can expect the barriers to go down, and not always then!

Planting new churches has been a major emphasis in recent years among all the major denominations in Britain. For many, this is the way forward for reaching new people and building new congregations. It is seen as a very effective form of evangelism.

Spurgeon's College and Oasis Trust are placing teams of mainly young people in under-churched areas of East London. They live and work in the area, getting involved in youth clubs, football clubs

[3] Darrell Jackson, article in the *Baptist Times*, 7 November, 2002.

and community activities. They worship in homes, but refuse the term church till it is given to them and owned by local people. One group didn't give themselves any name, but waited for people in the area to name them. The name their neighbours eventually settled on, Cable Street Community Church, came as a surprise. Here is one bottom-up approach to church planting which could be a model for the future.[4]

The purpose-driven church

Instead of being driven or motivated by various needs such as finance and keeping the buildings in good repair, the purpose-driven church says that a healthy church will place equal emphasis on five biblical purposes: knowing Christ, growing in Christ, serving Christ, sharing Christ and worshipping through Christ. Thousands of churches around the world are building around these purposes, but in relation to their own culture.

One example of this kind of church is a newly planted church in New York City. The church was planted almost immediately after, and because of, the events of 11th September 2001, and is called The Journey. It is a casual, contemporary Christian church designed for the New York City lifestyle.

To begin with the church consisted of only 15 to 20 people. After Easter 2002 weekly worship services were started in a theatre that could accommodate 110 people. By the end of the year they had outgrown that theatre and in early 2003 moved into a larger 400-seat theatre. The focus is on building relationships. The philosophy is to talk openly about relationships, to use technology to aid spiritual growth, to play together by going to the cinema, theatre or sporting events, to use the arts to worship and celebrate God, and to talk about work, life and the next steps in a relationship with God.

---

[4] Stuart Murray and Anne Wilkinson-Hayes, quoted in Michael Moynagh, *Changing World, Changing Church* (Monarch Books, 2001), p. 109.

The church's objectives are to help people experience God, to grow in community, to pursue faith, to redefine church for people, and to offer a support network for people at various stages of their life. Examples of the way these objectives are achieved include Free Lunch Fridays for students and faculty from New York University, Free Rush Hour Breakfast outreach events for young professionals on their way to work, and a coffee house that offers live bands and free beverages and snacks each evening from 9.00 pm to 11.30 pm.

The church encourages people to join growth groups to study subjects such as experiencing God and seeing things from a Christian perspective. 'Thank God it's Monday' is aimed at helping people to see their job as part of their life's purpose, and 'Making Love Last Forever' is a group for married couples.

The cell church

'Cell church' is the term used to describe a church that meets primarily in small groups, either in a home, at work, or in a school or college. The cells belong together as a local church. In some instances there is less emphasis on attendance at a central meeting. The main emphasis is on attending the small group meeting during the week. The movement was originated by Ralph Neighbour in Houston, Texas, and it rapidly gained worldwide recognition. Some of its key biblical values are to develop genuine community, evangelise through the multiplication of cells, encourage discipleship and involvement through every member in ministry. Apparently this model has been particularly effective in Anglican churches and new church plants.

There are three main forms of cell church. First, there is G12. This form of cell church believes that just as Jesus was given twelve disciples, God has twelve people for each believer to influence and disciple through prayer and example. Each believer, over a period of time, becomes a leader and finds up to twelve other people to disciple. These become the Group of

12 or G12 Cell. London City Church and Kensington Temple are UK examples of G12.

Cell UK is another expression of cell church. Again, the emphasis is on everybody being involved, lifestyle evangelism, growing disciples, leadership training, and pastoral care for each person in the group. On their website, Cell UK describe their background as follows:

> In the mid-90s, Laurence Singlehurst, then Director of Youth With A Mission England, heard Ralph Neighbour speak on cell church during a trip to India. Laurence was profoundly affected by the vision and values of cell church and consequently invited Ralph to speak in the UK. In 1995, the first British National Cell Conference took place in Harpenden and was attended by 250 church leaders from different church backgrounds. This enthusiastic beginning and the need to provide those church leaders with resources gave birth to Cell UK, as an organisation to serve the cell church movement. Originally a department of Youth With A Mission, Cell UK is now an independent organisation and charity in its own right.

The third form of cell church is the so-called house church. The house church movement has a lesser emphasis than some other models on the larger celebration.

As with all forms of Church there are strengths and weaknesses in all three styles of cell church. Elements of the cell church movement can be seen in both the seeker and the purpose-driven movements. It is interesting also to note elements of the seeker and purpose-driven models in the cell church. For example, the G12 asks for an understanding of four statements:

1. My life has a purpose, and that purpose is to win souls for Jesus.
2. I fulfil my purpose best as part of a cell in a G12 cell church.
3. I will never be satisfied in life until I fulfil my God-given purpose.

4. I have no promise of tomorrow. If I don't fulfil my purpose today I may never fulfil it at all.

There is evidence that the cell church movement is one of the biggest church movements in the world today.

Natural church development

There is international interest in the principles of 'natural church development', particularly from smaller churches. Churches in Brazil, Croatia, Denmark, France, Germany, The Netherlands, Russia, Switzerland, Latin America, the USA and the UK have benefited from implementing the principles of NCD.

Christian Schwarz lists 'eight essential qualities of healthy churches'.

1. Empowering leadership.
2. Gift-orientated ministry.
3. Passionate spirituality.
4. Functional structures.
5. Inspiring worship services.
6. Holistic small groups.
7. Need-orientated evangelism.
8. Loving relationships.

He adds, 'No church wanting to grow qualitatively and quantitatively can afford to overlook any one of these eight quality characteristics.'[5]

Common principles

One of the most encouraging signs is to see certain common principles in all four of the movements described above, and to

---

[5] Christian Schwarz, *Natural Church Development* (Church Smart Resources, 1996).

see how much local church initiatives incorporate some of these principles.

Creativity and variety abound. In the USA, Leith Anderson identifies the emerging shopping-centre church. Just as the American shopping mall offers variety, convenience and anonymity, and for those who want it identification (regular customers are recognised and their names may be on mailing lists) so some churches are doing the same. Anderson offers further examples:

> Hope Chapel in Hermosa Beach, California, started as a surfer church, holding services on the beach. It changed to become a shopping-centre church, offering more than sixty identified ministries including jogging, skiing, special programmes for victims of substance abuse, a divorce-recovery ministry and van service for the disabled.
>
> Central Presbyterian Church in St. Louis, Missouri, has a 'Lucy Programme' (named after the Peanuts cartoon where Lucy plays the psychiatrist), providing counsel and spiritual help for children. The target group is kindergartners through high schoolers whose parents are alcoholic or divorcing.[6]

After listing many varieties of church, Anderson says, 'There is something for almost everyone. These shopping-centre churches have looked around to determine the needs and interests of those they want to reach and provided some type of relevant programme or ministry.' Some might argue, Anderson says, that these churches 'have abandoned their central mission of making disciples for Jesus Christ. In most cases they have not.' These churches 'have gone to such variety out of a powerful motivation for ministry and evangelism'.

The American researcher George Barna identifies some other ways of being church:[7]

---

[6] Leith Anderson, *A Church for the 21st Century* (Bethany House Publishers, 1992), p. 167.

[7] Quoted in *Quadrant*, May 2002.

- Cyberchurch – perhaps 10–20 per cent of Americans will find their spiritual 'home' on the Internet.
- Event church – infrequent, community-wide worship events with no long-term commitment.
- Boutique church – providing only one dimension of ministry (worship, or discipleship, or some other dimension).
- Communal church – a revival of shared living.
- Compassion clusters – coupling belief and social action in service rather than worship.
- Prayer shelters – focusing on praying together.
- Marketplace ministries – 'church' in the workplace instead of bringing work colleagues to church.

In the UK there are many examples and models of creativity. A Baptist church in Grays, Essex, faithfully serves those outside the church by providing clothing for families in need. This is such a strong feature that the church has become known as 'the church with the black sack ministry'. They also provide holidays for single-parent families, many of whom are referred to the church by social services and other agencies.

It is not only times and venues for worship that are changing, but also styles of worship. Some churches mix sixth-century liturgy with alternative rock, monastic visual images with high technology, and early Christian traditions with post-modern culture.

But it's not all change!

The letter at the beginning of this chapter shows that change is not always popular. The well-known broadcaster, David Frost, once said that the great British public like a church not to go to. There was evidence for this in a television series shown on Channel 4 in November 2002 called *The English Church*. The church was described as 'the true museum of the country'.

At the beginning of the twenty-first century, the Christian church in the UK is a mixture of contrasts. The tragic news is that the number of people who go to church once a month or more has dropped from 10.9 per cent in 1980 to 9.5 per cent in 1990 and then to 7.5 per cent in 2003. The situation is even more serious when we take into account the age of many regular churchgoers and the absence of children and youth in so many churches. However, a significant number of churches are growing, particularly black-majority churches.

Be ready to learn from any church

Everyone knows there is no such thing as a perfect church, but if you look hard enough, there is something to be learned from nearly every church. No one church is totally right. And no one church is totally wrong. Most churches manage to do something well, and it is worth looking hard below the surface to find out what this is.

Sadly, some churches, mainly larger ones, seem unwilling to learn from other churches, particularly ones smaller than they are. There is a strong pride factor present in these churches. They feel threatened at the thought of learning from others. Surely others are looking at them as models? They feel they should be the originators of new ideas. This kind of pride prevents some churches from growing into healthy, biblical communities. The truth is, we can let go our pride and be prepared and open enough to learn something from all of them, even if it's what they learned through their mistakes.

There is no one secret key to church growth

There is a tendency among some Christians to think that there is only one way of being church. They find an effective model and assume it will work for them. For example, if some find a church that acts effectively as an agent for social action, the tendency is to think that is the way all churches should go. Others will see church in terms of a worshipping community, so worship is very high on the agenda and other things are over-looked. Still others will see church as evangelism and being seeker-centred, so winning people to Christ is their priority to the exclusion of all else.

The temptation is to follow our own personal preferences. In Acts 2 we have a description of the first church:

> They joined with the other believers and devoted themselves to the apostles' teaching and fellowship, sharing in the Lord's Supper and in prayer. A deep sense of awe came over them all, and the apostles performed many miraculous signs and wonders. And all the believers met together constantly and shared everything they had. They sold their possessions and shared the proceeds with those in need. They worshiped together at the Temple each day, met in homes for the Lord's Supper, and shared their meals with great joy and generosity – all the while praising God and enjoying the goodwill of all the people. And each day the Lord added to their group those who were being saved. (Acts 2:42–47, NLT)

Many leaders fix on just one of the functions of the first church and believe it to be the answer to decline. For example, people say that miraculous signs and wonders are what is needed. Others have said that we need teaching and fellowship. Still others have focused on communal living, sharing our possessions or selling them and giving the proceeds to the poor. Others focus on worship and believe that is what is needed. But it is misleading to think that just one function might be the key to spiritual revival and attracting people to church.

The reality is that the strongest and healthiest and most effective churches are focusing on all the functions described in Acts 2, and that is called balance. So how do we bring such balance to our local churches?

2
Healthy Churches Are Built on Purpose

It has been said that it's easy for a church to be a mile wide and an inch deep. Some churches try to do too much and spread themselves too thinly. Each church should get to know its unique purpose, and that will come from understanding the biblical principles and functions on which it must build in order to be a Bible-based church. This is called balance.

The Jerusalem church in Acts 2 is the biblical model. It is clear that the church practised discipleship ('They . . . devoted themselves to the apostles' teaching'). They were also a fellowship ('. . . and fellowship'). Worship was a key function ('They worshiped together at the Temple each day, met in homes for the Lord's Supper'). Serving one another and the community was high on their agenda ('And all the believers met together constantly and shared everything they had. They sold their possessions and shared the proceeds with those in need'). Evangelism was taking place ('And each day the Lord added to their group those who were being saved').

Balance is also implied in Ephesians 4:11–12: 'It was he who gave some to be apostles, some to be prophets, some to be evangelists, and some to be pastors and teachers, to prepare God's people for works of service, so that the body of Christ may be built up.' Although theologians and scholars may discuss what is meant by the terms 'apostle' and 'prophet', this list of church leaders implies a balanced church. Leaders with different gifts equip the members of the church so that the needed ministries can be carried out. Imagine the church where the members are prepared and equipped for ministry by a gifted team of apostles, prophets, evangelists, pastors and teachers. It would certainly be a balanced church made up of balanced believers. The objective? 'So that the body of Christ may be built up.' The healthiest churches are balanced churches.

Wherever your church is located, whether it is an established church or a newly planted one, be sure to find its unique purpose through studying the principles and functions of Acts 2, Ephesians 4 and other New Testament passages.

In Acts 2 it seems as though the church had everything together. But like any church, there were weaknesses. One weakness came to the surface and we read about it in Acts 6:1. As the church grew, 'there were rumblings of discontent. Those who spoke Greek complained against those who spoke Hebrew, saying that their widows were being discriminated against in the daily distribution of food' (NLT). So the twelve apostles called a meeting of believers to consider what might be done:

> 'We apostles should spend our time preaching and teaching the word of God, not administering a food program,' they said. 'Now look around among yourselves, brothers, and select seven men who are well respected and are full of the Holy Spirit and wisdom. We will put them in charge of this business. Then we can spend our time in prayer and preaching and teaching the word.' (Acts 6:2–4, NLT)

Notice that the apostles did not allow themselves to be diverted from certain functions that were essential to the church. Not only is this a warning to leaders to guard against being distracted or diverted by very deserving needs, but it is a reminder to all church members that there are certain functions that have to be accomplished if a church is to be a church. Notice also the result here: the church was set free to continue its mission. A barrier to its growth and development was removed and the apostles were vindicated: 'God's message was preached in ever-widening circles. The number of believers greatly increased in Jerusalem, and many of the Jewish priests were converted, too' (Acts 6:7, NLT).

Whatever pattern or model of church you choose, the strongest churches are those that are balanced according to biblical principles and functions. The alternative is to become a church that tries to do everything, or one that is led in only one direction, usually dictated by the leader's particular passion, or by the passion and heart of a group within the church, or even by one influential member of the congregation.

Balance brings unity

Ephesians 4 stresses the importance of unity in the body of Christ: 'Be completely humble and gentle; be patient, bearing with one another in love. Make every effort to keep the unity of the Spirit through the bond of peace' (Ephesians 4:2–3). A sense of purpose creates unity. A church without purpose either tries to travel in too many directions at once, or does the opposite and remains stationary. Even worse, it can easily become fragmented. Lack of purpose creates frustration and frustration creates confusion and division. Imagine the scene in a PCC or church meeting where people are trying to 'jump start' a stationary church by suggesting an overwhelming number of ways forward, none of which gain approval.

Paul tells the Philippian church, 'Make my joy complete by being like-minded, having the same love, being one in spirit and purpose' (Philippians 2:2). Incorporating balance will help to bring unity of purpose. People know where they are going. They get a sense of being on the same team because they have common goals and objectives. They may have differing viewpoints on how those objectives are to be reached, but because they believe their church is going somewhere, they pull together. There is a greater sense of belonging. In the believers' prayer described in Acts 4:23–31, unity of fellowship is strongly expressed: 'They raised their voices together in prayer to God' (v. 24). They prayed for a number of common objectives: 'Consider their threats and enable your servants to speak your word with great boldness. Stretch out your hand to heal and perform miraculous signs and wonders through the name of your holy servant Jesus' (vv. 29–30). The result? 'All the believers were one in heart and mind' (v. 32). There was unity of fellowship because they owned common objectives.

Balance encourages mission

Your church members will understand that mission, and evangelism in particular, is a process. It starts by engaging the community and moves on to discipling new believers, incorporating them into the church family and equipping them for their own mission and ministry. Church members will see that their church is engaged in a process, and they will understand something that has largely been forgotten in UK churches: there is something to bring people to! Because the church has seriously declined and been seen to be totally irrelevant by many people, and because many present-day Christians feel guilty about not engaging the culture, they have concentrated on 'going out into the world' to the exclusion of bringing people back into God's family, the church. Christian congregations have been influenced to believe that unbelievers cannot be expected to come to church any more. The message from many pulpits has been that Christians must go out to where the people are. That's good. That's as it should be, but not to the exclusion of bringing people back into the local church family. Christians have been told to go out into the world, when the truth is that most of them are there already, but they don't always know what to say or how to say it. Have you sent people out from your church, but failed to equip them? How well are you equipping people in your church for mission?

Mark Greene, Executive Director of the London Institute for Contemporary Christianity, writes:

> By and large, the Church has not fully envisioned, equipped, or supported its people to reach out to others where they are. We have often failed to give existing (church) members a compelling vision of what it means to live as whole-life disciples of Jesus in the modern world. Opportunities abound, however. Imagine if the people we already have in church were envisioned, equipped and supported. Imagine if we were taught how to be good news to the people with whom we already have relationships. Imagine if we grasped the impact that showing and sharing the love of Christ could have.[1]

For a whole variety of reasons, Christians have lost confidence in inviting their friends, neighbours and work colleagues to church. They realise that while the church may meet their needs, it won't meet their neighbours' needs. The apostles went out, as commanded by Christ, and on the Day of Pentecost they proclaimed the good news on the streets, but notice that 'about three thousand were added to their number' (Acts 2:41). And the following verses tell us what they were added to: teaching, fellowship, worship, home groups, prayer, sharing together and further mission.

The parable of the great banquet in Luke 14 and Matthew 22 focuses on God's invitation to 'come' to what God has prepared: 'Come, for everything is now ready' (Luke 14:17). Jesus uses an invitation to a banquet as a sign of God's grace. In the parable the servants are commanded: 'Go out quickly into the streets and alleys of the town and bring in the poor, the crippled, the blind and the lame' (14:21).

---

[1] Mark Greene, *Idea* magazine, March/April 2003, p. 8.

There are two principles in the parable. One has been observed, the other has been neglected. Quite correctly believers have been encouraged to 'go' out into the world, but churches have neglected the need to invite people to 'come' into the family of God, the church. In the parable, everything was 'ready' for those who were to be invited. Often our churches are not ready, so we don't have the confidence, or see the need, to invite people to come. Jesus tells the disciples to go, but with the clear command not just to tell people, but to 'make disciples . . . baptising them . . . teaching them' – in other words to incorporate them into the family of God (Matthew 28:19–20). Because we have neglected to do this, many local churches have become places for believers and not unbelievers; for the saved and not the sinners; for the found and not the lost; for the well and not the sick; for the healed and not the broken. The church exists for those who are not yet in it, but all too often we want to keep it for ourselves. People shouted mockingly at Jesus, 'He saved others, but he can't save himself!' What they shouted was true. And as the principle was true for Jesus, so it is for his church. We cannot save ourselves if we would save others.

Clearly if we want to see people come in, then believers must have confidence to invite people in. Some big changes will have to take place in many churches – mainly in the way they think about church. Bringing balance to the church in terms of biblical functions is a big step in the right direction. If you are faithful enough to *go* out into all the world and invite people into the family of God, then what you invite them into is all-important. As is sometimes said, 'You only get one opportunity to make a first impression on an unchurched person.'

Balance helps to focus the teaching ministry of the church

One of the advantages of using a lectionary is that it prevents clergy from only preaching their particular passion. However, the question needs to be asked, 'Does following the Lectionary actually enable a local church to address all the issues unique to itself and its community?' Jesus didn't preach on certain subjects because of the calendar, but because of the need. There is generally a great fear of preaching to felt needs, but isn't that what Jesus did? Felt needs are often the clues to real needs. Peter Brooks, a respected BBC broadcaster and religious producer, said more than 20 years ago, 'We need to speak to their felt needs in such a way as to reach through them to deeper needs than ever they have been aware of.'

If your church wants to be a fully functioning biblical community – a biblically balanced church – then try to address issues relating to the core values and principles relevant to your particular church. This does not mean ignoring certain sections of the Bible, but it does mean teaching the Bible in the light of current issues. The teaching and preaching will reflect the biblical balance your church is aiming for. This means the leaders, perhaps in consultation with the congregation, will ask the following types of question: 'What are the subjects/issues God wants us to address this year?' 'Where are we on our journey as a local church at this time?' 'Are we including both Old and New Testament passages throughout the year?' 'What are the needs and priorities to be addressed in the lives of the individuals that make up our particular congregation?'

In the church I currently pastor, the pastoral team spends time in prayer and discussion each November/December asking these kinds of question. The result is a number of sermon series we believe we should plan for the coming year. These series hopefully reflect a balanced approach, and are publicised on a simple bookmark. Church members are encouraged to keep the bookmark and pray about sermon series through the year. No dates or lengths of sermon series are mentioned until nearer the time. Because they know the subjects that are going to be addressed, the church members know which services are 'safe' to bring their unchurched friends to. Our approach is to ensure that we preach a series of messages from both Old and New Testaments, a series once a year on relationships, including marriage and parenting, and another on topical themes that we believe are relevant to where we are as a church at any particular time. As with the Lectionary, nothing is fixed in concrete, and changes are sometimes made in the light of local, national and world events or issues.

Balance helps to guard against personal preferences

Everyone has preferences, particularly Christians when it comes to church. There are many styles of worship and church government. This is not wrong. What is wrong is when personal preferences begin to dominate.

Take the obvious example of worship. In a church of 500 members there are hundreds of personal preferences about style of worship. In a church of 50 members, or even as I once heard in a church of half a dozen members, personal preferences can dominate. How well I remember being at a conference where a vicar was weeping and physically exhausted by the pressure of the personal preferences coming from his tiny rural congregation about what their church should be. It's hard to resist such pressure.

Why does such pressure exist? It exists because a congregation has failed to understand that a church is not to be driven by personal preference, but by God's purposes. Another way of putting it is that your church is not there to satisfy the needs of established believers, but to be a balanced biblical community that reaches out to your local neighbourhood and beyond. The church needs to ask: 'What are we here for? What is our purpose?'

Balance is the key to health. It helps to define purpose. It brings unity. It stimulates and encourages mission. It helps to focus the teaching ministry of the church and it delivers us from being guided by personal preferences. The church's purpose and mission is clear. It is called to praise and glorify God, to establish Christ's kingdom and to make disciples throughout the world. This will not happen effectively if the people in your church are divided over their understanding of purpose, or in how to reach the unchurched and disciple new believers, or are following their own preferences.

Balance does not mean complacency

There are many historical and contemporary examples of a balanced approach to church life and ministry. In earlier years, under the inspiration of leaders like John Wesley and George Whitefield, many churches in Britain and the United States were spiritually awakened to become biblically balanced churches. Under the impact of the spiritual awakening, many new churches were planted – churches that were biblically based and culturally relevant. In those churches the gospel was proclaimed in ways that were understood. Community work flourished. Prisons, hospitals, working conditions and the care of children were influenced and reformed. In London during the nineteenth century, Spurgeon's Tabernacle grew to become a large church of thousands, which reached and discipled thousands of Londoners, established an orphanage and pioneered education.

Many contemporary churches are also committed to changing community conditions for the better. One of the strongest examples is the Saddleback Community Church in Orange County, California. Here is a balanced church exercising a well-rounded ministry that impacts the community. Thousands of people attend every Saturday and Sunday to worship and then throw themselves into community service through the life of their church. The results are phenomenal. In a ministry called Celebrate Recovery, people are recovering from life situations. This church has a huge support ministry for a whole range of life experiences from addiction to serious illness, bereavement and relationship issues. A balanced church will give attention to social needs, just as the church did in Acts.

Most churches need a significant move of the Holy Spirit and a radical change of mindset before the membership can be enlisted to meet the needs of people in a holistic fashion. The first step is to try and understand and come to grips with what the community needs.

Churches need to plan as well as pray, but many do not take thoughtful planning and strategy as seriously as they might. Churches that mobilise their membership usually grow. They equip workers for ministry and mission, and church members learn the thrill of serving Christ effectively.

Some Christians think that planning is unspiritual, but Christian Schwarz says: 'Church growth in the power of the Holy Spirit does not mean ignoring God's principles. It means putting those principles to work in our churches as much as possible, even when they seem unusual, hard to follow, go against our tradition, or even hurt.'[2]

As a pilot, I know that to be lost in an aircraft is frightening. It happened once to me and it was one of the most terrifying moments of my life. Similarly, for a church to be lost in terms of its direction and purpose breeds division, frustration and fear.

The Bible supports planning: 'Those who plan what is good find love and faithfulness' (Proverbs 14:22). The story of Nehemiah rebuilding the wall of Jerusalem includes his careful planning as well as his praying. Jesus said, 'Suppose one of you wants to build a tower. Will he not first sit down and estimate the cost to see if he has enough money to complete it? For if he lays the foundation and is not able to finish it, everyone who sees it will ridicule him, saying, "This fellow began to build and was not able to finish"' (Luke 14:28–30).

---

[2] Christian Schwarz, *Natural Church Development* (Church Smart Resources, 1996), p. 126.

God is a planner. Some Christians use the phrase 'the plan of salvation'. Early in the ministry of Jesus, when the disciples found him in a solitary place, they said, "Everyone is looking for you!" Jesus replied, "Let us go somewhere else – to the nearby villages – so that I can preach there also. That is why I have come." So he travelled throughout Galilee, preaching in their synagogues and driving out demons' (Mark 1:37–39). Jesus would not be diverted from his mission.

> The tools of planning and goal-setting can be of tremendous benefit. They can be steps of faith; but they must be guided carefully by the hand of God.[3]

Yes, but how?

Begin by asking such questions as:

- What is the essential purpose of my church and how does it relate to the congregation and community?
- How should this purpose affect the aims and plans of my church, and does it actually do so?
- In the light of this purpose, what should be the aims of the congregation?
- Are the church members conscious of these aims? If not, why not?
- Do these aims govern the development of my church, its organisations and their functions? If not, why not?
- Are there definite long-, mid- and short-term goals for growth?
- Are the goals measurable and attainable?
- Are the goals and aims connected to the purpose of the church?

---

[3] Thom Rainer, *The Book of Church Growth* (Nashville: Broadman, 1993), p. 270.

As I mentioned in the Introduction to this book, in June 1987 I wrote in our church magazine the following five goals:

- To proclaim the gospel.
- To be a fellowship in which people can find God's love and forgiveness.
- To be a fellowship in which every member can be encouraged to grow.
- To be a fellowship which serves the community.
- To be a church that is a support base for mission and wider ministry.

I went on to say that we meet together each week:

- to celebrate the life of God;
- to cultivate personal growth in Christ;
- to care about one another;
- to communicate Christ to the world.

This was my attempt in those days to build a balanced church, and to a certain extent it happened. Today I would express it differently. I am still learning, and am grateful for God's patience with me over trying to build a balanced, healthy, growing church.

So what steps should you take to bring balance, health and growth to your church? How do you bring about change from narrow thinking to balanced thinking? How do you build a biblically balanced church?

Begin by identifying the strengths and weaknesses of your church in the light of the New Testament principles and purposes for the church. Is the sense of belonging (fellowship) in your church strong or weak? Is the process of discipling new believers strong or weak? Is the process for identifying the gifts of church members and involving them in ministry strong or weak? Is evangelism a strength or a weakness in your church?

Is worship attracting unbelievers, or is it just for believers? Is the church united in its mission and purpose, or is it fragmented?

Every church has its strengths and weaknesses and making an honest appraisal of these is an excellent first step towards preparing for change and becoming a healthier church.

3

Preparing for Change

If you're the team leader in your church, preparation for change begins with you. Please accept this responsibility, because your church is unlikely to change unless you personally are prepared to change. Some congregations are frustrated because their leader or leaders are unwilling to change.

Spend time studying, reflecting and praying. Unless you are willing to give time to knowing God's purpose and how to fulfil it, intentional change probably won't happen. A new vision for the local church comes from the heart of the leader, which is why many churches today invite their clergy to take sabbaticals. Some denominations strongly advise their ministers to take a three-month sabbatical every seven years. If you are the team leader – pastor, vicar, minister, elder – this is a great opportunity to spend time reflecting, studying and praying about your own ministry and the life and ministry of your church.

My three-month sabbatical in the autumn of 1997 was the beginning of a journey of change in my own life, as well as in the life of the church I pastor. The sense of God's vision for our church which I developed over that time was shared with the other leaders of the church, who continued to reflect and pray. The vision was then gradually unpacked and shared with the church. There are no short cuts or quick fixes.

The process

Dan Southerland, who led his church through immense change from being an established, traditional church for believers, to a growing church for both unbelievers and believers, describes five steps in the process of preparing for change.[1] These are drawn from Nehemiah 1. Nehemiah was a visionary leader.

1. Collect information

> The words of Nehemiah son of Hacaliah: In the month of Kislev in the twentieth year, while I was in the citadel of Susa, Hanani, one of my brothers, came from Judah with some other men, and I questioned them about the Jewish remnant that survived the exile, and also about Jerusalem. They said to me, 'Those who survived the exile and are back in the province are in great trouble and disgrace. The wall of Jerusalem is broken down, and its gates have been burned with fire.' (Nehemiah 1:1–3)

Notice how Nehemiah gathered as much information as he could.

2. Holy discontent with the status quo

> When I heard these things, I sat down and wept. (Nehemiah 1:4)

Southerland reminds us, 'Vision is usually birthed out of heartache and burden. It must come from the heart.'

3. Fasting

> For some days I mourned and fasted and prayed before the God of heaven. (Nehemiah 1:4)

Southerland says, 'Vision is usually birthed out of a serious search for God's direction.'

---

[1] Dan Southerland, *Transitioning* (Zondervan, 2000), p. 25.

4. Pray

The depth of Nehemiah's commitment is reflected in this prayer.

> 'O Lord, God of heaven, the great and awesome God, who keeps his covenant of love with those who love him and obey his commands, let your ear be attentive and your eyes open to hear the prayer your servant is praying before you day and night for your servants, the people of Israel. I confess the sins we Israelites, including myself and my father's house, have committed against you.' (Nehemiah 1:5–6)

He ends the prayer with these words from verse 11, 'O Lord, let your ear be attentive to the prayer of this your servant and to the prayer of your servants who delight in revering your name. Give your servant success today by granting him favour in the presence of this man.'

5. Wait

There is a four-month time lapse between chapters 1 and 2. Southerland says, 'Vision is usually given to those who wait patiently for it.' Time spent in deliberate preparation is never wasted time.

I commend those five steps. The story of Nehemiah is an outstanding example of good leadership and how to go about change. For the purpose of this particular book, here are a number of practical steps under three headings.

1. Study

Relevant Bible passages

Take time out to study sections of the Bible that have to do with leadership. The story of Nehemiah is a good place to begin. Also study sections of the Bible related to the church. Read through the book of Acts and make a note of principles that apply to any church, anywhere, at any time. Allow God to speak to you through the Bible about your own church. Read everything in the Bible that has to do with God's purposes for his people and the way he chooses to operate in the world through the church. The following extracts from Ephesians are some examples:

His intent was that now, through the church, the manifold wisdom of God should be made known to the rulers and authorities in the heavenly realms, according to his eternal purpose which he accomplished in Christ Jesus our Lord. (Ephesians 3:10–11)

Consequently, you are no longer foreigners and aliens, but fellow-citizens with God's people and members of God's household, built on the foundation of the apostles and prophets, with Christ Jesus himself as the chief cornerstone. In him the whole building is joined together and rises to become a holy temple in the Lord. And in him you too are being built together to become a dwelling in which God lives by his Spirit. (Ephesians 2:19–22)

Now to him who is able to do immeasurably more than all we ask or imagine, according to his power that is at work within us, to him be glory in the church and in Christ Jesus throughout all generations, for ever and ever! (Ephesians 3:20–21)

The whole letter to the Ephesian believers has so much to say about the church. Study this section of the New Testament along with the other epistles and make a note of every relevant verse or statement. These sections of Scripture may have been read many times before, but perhaps not in such an intentional way with your own church in mind.

Keep a journal of what you believe God is saying to you so that you can further test it and eventually share it with other leaders in your church.

Information

Collect and study information about your church and the surrounding community. How long has this church been in existence? Why was it started? Who started it? Why is it located where it is? What has been its journey so far, it's history? What has been its previous philosophy of church and understanding of mission? Chart its progress through the years in terms of growth and decline. Answers to these questions will give clues to the congregation's expectations of the future. Are those expectations correct? Can they be changed? Should they be changed?

Moving on to the community, define the geographical dimensions of the community, either by the parish boundary or by distance from the church. What is the predominant age group of the community? Provide a breakdown of the age groups. Are you in a relatively new community or an old established one? How has the community changed? Compare past needs with present ones. Describe its general culture and subculture. Identify and describe the community needs that should be met by the church. What future needs can be anticipated and prepared for?

Spend time collecting information about your own church and community, about other churches in your community and well beyond. This is more easily done these days through the Internet. A local council Internet site will often show a breakdown of the community in terms of age groups, number of people employed locally, number unemployed, and how these figures have changed in recent years. The changes will indicate certain trends. The same, or similar, information would no doubt be available at a local library.

The local council Internet site will include the Community Strategy for your area. This is a highly important document prepared by the Local Strategic Partnership, consisting of various organisations in the community. Is your church, or network of local churches, represented in this partnership?

Another helpful site for community information is National Statistics Online – Census 2001. Visit www.statistics.gov.uk/census 2001/ for population statistics and plenty of other information here about your community.

Books

Read as many books as possible on church health and growth. Read about and visit other churches. Gather information about them, such as how they go about their ministry and mission. Find churches that are effective in reaching the unchurched and find out how they do it. Don't copy their methods (though they may have some good ideas), but learn from their principles.

Plan to be a healthy church. 'That comes through a process of comparison, consultation, and self-evaluation. Comparison is made with other churches, especially healthy ones. Consultations with outsiders helps us to see ourselves as others see us. Self-evaluation is applying insiders' insights to the comparison and consultations.'[2]

Warning: There is a tendency for some leaders and congregational members to read the latest book or attend the latest seminar on being church, and then wait for the next book or seminar, without making a commitment to change or actually implementing anything that has been learned. This might be because some leaders are not gifted or skilled in implementation and need help. We should never stop reading, but there comes a time when we must put into action whatever is necessary to make the local church more healthy and effective. To read countless books and do nothing is like reading the Bible but never applying its message to our lives.

So having studied Bible passages, collected information

---

[2] Leith Anderson, *A Church for the 21st Century* (Bethany House Publishers, 1992), p. 128.

about the church and the community, and read through some books written by experienced practitioners, what's the next step?

2. Reflect

Reflect with a view to action. Hopefully, you will now have a document containing information. Some of that information will begin to guide you toward a strategy for building a healthy, balanced church.

Part of the process of establishing vision and direction for the local church must be an openness to learn from others. Sadly, as we have seen, there is sometimes resistance to learning from others, particularly other churches. Pride and an unwillingness to learn from others or to try new things stop the process. This kind of pride often expresses itself in very subtle ways. For example, 'That idea wouldn't work here, because we're in a very different situation' can sometimes mean, 'Because we didn't think of it first, we're not going to use it.' Sometimes churches are closed to a new idea because they don't want to feel any sense of obligation towards another church.

Worst of all, some 'successful' and well-known churches are afraid of learning from others. They think, 'We're a church of long standing. What will others think of us if they know the idea didn't originate with us? They expect us to be original!' It's a humbling thing for some 'successful' churches to say they are implementing something they learned from another church, particularly one that is smaller. Larger churches sometimes look down on smaller churches (as well as some smaller churches sometimes looking down on larger ones).

'All leaders are learners', says Rick Warren, and 'the moment you stop learning is the moment you stop leading.' Don't let pride get in the way of honest reflection and a willingness to learn from others.

Reflection should be carried out prayerfully, as was the case with Nehemiah. Ask God to help you form a strategy, a plan for change. Our plans need to come from God. Some people worry that planning precludes the sovereignty of God and the leadership of the Holy Spirit. On the contrary, prayer, dependence on the Holy Spirit and careful reading of Scripture will reveal God's plans for your church. The fact is that churches which plan for growth usually experience growth.

Peter Wagner lists six reasons for planning:[3]

1. It increases efficiency. God's resources of time, energy and money are best used for good stewardship.
2. It permits mid-course corrections.
3. It unites the team with a singular plan and vision. Each member of the team understands his or her role in the vision.
4. It helps measure effectiveness. Progress is measured according to the plans.
5. It makes accountability natural.
6. It can become a model to help others.

Strategies for spiritual and numerical growth that focus on building up the health of the church may sound businesslike. They may not be biblical in the literal sense, but they are not unbiblical in that they derive their inspiration and motivation from the Bible and are based on God's desire for his church to grow. 'The tools of planning and goal-setting can be of tremendous benefit. They can be steps of faith; but they must be guided carefully by the hand of God.'[4]

The process of reflection will hopefully end with a paper containing a suggested strategy for health and growth.

---

[3] Peter Wagner, *Strategies for Church Growth* (Regal, 1987), pp. 32–34.
[4] Thom Rainer, *The Book of Church Growth* (Nashville: Broadman, 1993), p. 270

3. Pray

If anything is going to happen, there must be a commitment, and that commitment is first expressed through prayer.

Prayer was at the heart of church life in Acts: they prayed before they selected and appointed leaders, they prayed during times of persecution, they prayed for the progress of the gospel, they prayed for the sick, they prayed for church leaders and workers, they prayed for the church, and they prayed for the community and the world.

Prayer demonstrates our dependence on God. Even after Pentecost the church showed their dependence on God through prayer. We cannot build churches in our own strength. We might be able to build organisations and institutions, but only God can build the church. If we neglect prayer, we neglect the power source behind all church health and growth.

When Peter Wagner began researching the spiritual dimensions of churches he was led into a much deeper understanding of the role of prayer in church growth.[5] By 1992, he had published three books on the subject. George Barna, in his study of some rapidly growing churches in America, found that prayer was the foundational ministry of these churches. They emphasised prayer in at least four major areas.

First, church members were given consistent Bible teaching about the importance of prayer in the Christian life. Teaching in sermons and the various programmes and ministries of the church encouraged prayer. There was little doubt in the mind of the average church member that prayer was a priority.

Second, the church leaders, beginning with the pastor, modelled dynamic prayer lives. Large segments of time were devoted to prayer despite busy schedules. Some pastors spent more time praying about their sermons than preparing them.

---

[5] C. Peter Wagner, *How to Have a Healing Ministry Without Making Your Church Sick* (Regal, 1987).

Third, the rapidly growing churches learned that praise for answered prayer was an integral part of prayer itself. The people learned that prayer really is effective as they heard about the many answers.

Fourth, growing churches engendered accountability for prayer. The prayer life of members, the prayer ministries of the church and the prayer life of church leaders were regularly held before the church.[6]

Prayer is indispensable to understanding God's vision for churches. Not only must we look beyond the world's ideas for vision, we must look beyond the visions of other churches. Though we can certainly learn from other growing churches, the vision God gives to one church is not the same as He gives to another church. As we pray to God for a vision for our churches, He will miraculously open our eyes to possibilities . . . the prayers of the early church unleashed the power of God to add thousands to the church. It happened then. It is happening in churches today. And it can happen in your church.[7]

Pray for spiritual and numerical growth. It is God's will for his church to be healthy.

---

[6] George Barna, *User Friendly Churches* (Regal, 1991).
[7] Thom Rainer, *The Book of Church Growth* (Nashville: Broadman, 1993), pp. 178, 184.

4

Communicating the Vision

There is a right time to share the vision. In your excitement and enthusiasm, you can share it too soon – possibly before it is fully formed, or before the rest of the church is ready to receive it. The way it is communicated also needs thought and preparation. Perhaps it is too much to share the whole vision at one time. Some church leaders have been disappointed, and even given up, because the members were unreceptive to the vision. It was too much too soon. Avoid making the vision complicated for people to understand. Keep it simple. Sharing in one session what has taken months for you to build is more than a congregation can assimilate.

The story of Nehemiah shows there is a right time to share the vision: 'I went to Jerusalem, and after staying there three days I set out during the night with a few men. I had not told anyone what my God had put in my heart to do for Jerusalem. There were no mounts with me except the one I was riding on' (Nehemiah 2:11–12). For some time Nehemiah kept the vision to himself. Share the dream too soon and some people will begin to tear it apart.

Share the vision with other members of the leadership team

Share the vision with others in leadership in your church. Take them through the process you went through. It is important that they too spend time in study, reflection and prayer. Encourage them to answer the same questions about what should be the purpose of the church. Is the church building on the functions described in Acts 2 and other relevant sections of the New Testament? Is the church tending to focus on only one or two functions? Help them to see the importance of balance, and how balance leads to health, and health to growth.

Consider such questions as: Is our church making disciples? Are we teaching our congregation about what it means to live as a follower of Jesus Christ in today's world? Is our worship sensitive to seekers? Do our people understand the purpose of our church – why we are here?

Work together to sharpen the vision. Help those who are cautious about the vision to understand and own it. Know the difference between dreamers and detailers. Both kinds of people are important to the process. Detailers can kill the dream by asking such questions as: How much will it cost? Who will do it? How long will it take? These might have been some of the reasons why Nehemiah didn't share his dream until it was fully formed. Dreamers, on the other hand, can have difficulty actually implementing the vision. Eventually they will need the detailers to make the vision a reality. The important principle is to work together.

Don't rush the process of sharing the vision and working on it together. The vision must be fully formed before taking it further. You will need to show your church that the vision has been thought about. That doesn't mean to say that others cannot ask questions about it. It doesn't mean that others cannot add to the dream. They can, and they can make it richer.

Share the vision with the next level of leaders

When the time is right, and when the main leadership team are in agreement, begin to share the vision with other leaders in the church. These will include leaders of departments and anyone with a leadership responsibility in the life and work of the church.

But how do you go about doing this? In Frinton Free Church we had a Leaders' Day. We spent the first half of the day setting out the vision. Our vision was built around the five principles of belonging, growing, serving, sharing and worshipping. They were also described as worship, evangelism, discipleship, fellowship and ministry – the five functions already identified in this book. Some churches identify six or eight functions. You must decide on the main building blocks of your vision. But keep it as simple as possible.

We arranged a simple exercise. We set out five circles of chairs in the church hall. We asked those who thought worship was the strongest element in our church to go and sit in one circle of chairs, and those who thought discipleship was the strongest element to go and sit in another circle of chairs. We had another circle for those who thought fellowship was the strongest, and circles for those who thought ministry or mission was the strongest. The result was interesting. We had most people sitting in the chairs marked worship and discipleship. The next group was ministry, the fourth group was mission and evangelism, and the fewest leaders of all sat in the circle of chairs marked fellowship! This simple exercise told us which areas of church life most of our leaders felt were the strongest.

We then asked the leaders to sit in the circle of chairs representing the area of church life and work they felt most passionate about. This time, the numbers in the circles were more evenly balanced. This told us that among our leaders we had people who had a heart for each of the five areas of church life that we felt were important. So why weren't we using these leaders in the areas they felt passionate about when God had provided us with leaders for all five functions?

The exercise visually made the point that our church needs to function equally in all five areas, and as a result our leaders were beginning to grasp the vision. Obviously the Leaders' Day was an opportunity for their input and questions, and for further prayer and reflection together.

The important principle here is to bring together all the leaders in the church so that they have the opportunity to understand and share in the vision-building process. This helps to build unity. Give time for questions to be asked and answered. This will help all your church leaders to become owners and carriers of the vision.

Communicate the vision to the whole church

Next comes the exciting process of beginning to share and communicate the vision to the whole church. Notice 'beginning' to share. Once again, take time over the process. Don't rush people. Share the vision in as many different ways as possible. People learn in different ways: some by hearing, some by reading and some by watching. Here are some of the ways in which to communicate the vision.

Through preaching

Don't underestimate the power of the pulpit. The pulpit is like the rudder of a ship. The best sermons are those that lead the church forward. Sermons are not just a one-off experience of worship. They are part of a spiritual journey, both as individuals and as a church. Part of the vision can be shared in every sermon.

At Flamingo Road Church in Fort Lauderdale, Florida, Dan Southerland preached three times through the book of Acts. On all three occasions he kept asking the question 'What is a New Testament church like?' One series of messages had these titles:

- How does a New Testament church pray? (Acts 1)
- How does a New Testament church fellowship? (Acts 2)
- How does a New Testament church worship? (Acts 2)
- How does a New Testament church give? (Acts 4)
- What do deacons do in a New Testament church? (Acts 6)
- How does a New Testament church do missions? (Acts 11)
- How does a New Testament church choose missionaries? (Acts 13)
- How does a New Testament church make decisions? (Acts 15)

Eventually one member of his congregation asked, 'We've been hearing about what it means to be a New Testament church, so when are we going to be one?' Isn't it great when members of the congregation feed the vision back to you in this way?

While on the staff of Frinton Free Church, for three years we took the first five Sundays of each new year and devoted one Sunday to each of the main functions of the church. On the first Sunday the preaching and worship theme for the day was membership and fellowship – the importance of belonging. The second Sunday was about discipleship, the third Sunday was about ministry and serving, the fourth Sunday was about mission and evangelism, and the fifth Sunday was about worship.

This is one of the ways to build vision and remind people of the main purposes and functions of a New Testament church, and it is much more biblical than going to the church meeting with a grand plan. Some churches have done this and it has been a disaster. A vision is something that comes to be owned not through a church meeting, but over a period of time, involving study, reflection and prayer. There is no need to go to a church meeting and take a vote on whether or not a church should worship, or serve, or evangelise, or have fellowship, or disciple people. These are givens. The vision is to help people realise the importance and priority of these functions and to remind them that the church needs to include all of them in an equal way. It is also a reminder that these functions do not happen automatically. There must be focus and intentionality. Preaching is not only about communicating information; it is about bringing transformation too. This means that the message must be well prepared. Among growing churches, pastors spend an average of 20 hours a week on sermon preparation!

Steve Chalke, a former associate pastor with me, writes:

> The big question a preacher should ask is not 'What should I preach about this Sunday?' but 'Where are we going as a church over the next 12 months, and how do we get there?' The majority of sermons should simply serve as a tool of this vision. In reality, a church with no strategic plan and direction will always be one that, in the final analysis, wastes the preaching opportunities presented to its leaders Sunday by Sunday. It's only when a church's leadership has carefully developed its strategy that it is in a position to determine the content of its preaching diary. Only after answering three key questions – 'Where are we?', 'Where are we going?' and 'How are we going to get there?' – is it possible to ascertain what you should be preaching and teaching about on a regular basis.[1]

Preaching the vision gives people time to understand and own it.

Through small groups

There are two ways of sharing the vision in small groups. One way is for key leaders to visit the groups and explain the vision more informally, providing people with an opportunity for

---

[1] Steve Chalke, *Alpha* magazine, July 1996, p. 23.

discussion and questions. The second way is to set up special groups to teach what the church is all about. Set up a discipleship group to teach discipleship. Set up a mission group to teach evangelism and mission. Set up a ministry group to teach about how to serve in and through the church. And set up a newcomers' group to teach about membership and fellowship to newcomers. The newcomers' group is also a great opportunity to teach new people the vision, strategy and philosophy of the church. They often grasp it more quickly than long-standing church members. And they are often far more enthusiastic. This is implementing the principle of building the church from the outside in. Soon a church may have more newcomers than longer serving members. That can present its own challenges, but some of the newcomers are the best adverts for the new vision.

Using small groups to share the vision is at the same time demonstrating the vision and purposes of the church. As people can begin to see the vision working, it is more difficult to argue against it.

Through a purpose statement

A purpose statement is another powerful tool for communicating vision. Try to condense the statement into a single sentence that can easily be remembered by the church membership. Don't make it so broad or vague that it is easily forgotten and becomes meaningless. Be specific. A good purpose statement is also measurable. It prompts you to ask if you are achieving it. It defines what you will do, and also what you will not do. It enables you to evaluate your church.

The following are examples of public purpose statements. They form a typical cross-section.

- 'Balham Baptist Church exists to worship God by showing the love of Jesus in action as well as words.'
- Jesmond Parish Church, Newcastle: 'We aim to glorify God

by being a worshipping, praying, serving and witnessing church, whose members seek to understand their faith more fully and to follow Christ more faithfully.'

- St Stephen's Church, Selly Park: 'St Stephen's church family exists to bring glory to God through following Jesus and serving others in the power of the Holy Spirit.'
- Hounslow Pentecostal Church: 'We seek to demonstrate God's love practically in the local community.'
- St George's Church, Leeds: 'To share the gospel, care for society and renew the church.'
- Lighthouse Christian Centre, Manchester: 'To serve God as we aim to reach out to those with both spiritual and material needs with the full gospel of our Lord Jesus Christ, nationally and internationally.'
- St Paul's, Howell Hill, Cheam: 'To be a church that connects people with Jesus Christ by leading them into membership of the body of Christ, strengthening them in spiritual maturity, equipping them for ministry, sending them out in mission, and doing all for God's magnification.'
- Rayleigh Baptist Church: 'To know Jesus and make him known.'

Make the purpose statement easily accessible. Put it on church literature as a constant reminder to everybody. At Frinton Free Church the statement is printed on a bookmark, and the bookmark is given to every person in each congregation over the first few Sundays of each new year. People are asked to keep the bookmark throughout the year as a reminder of what we believe to be God's purpose for the church. On one side of the bookmark is the purpose statement, and on the other side are the titles of the sermon series for the coming year. This serves three purposes. First, there is the reminder of the purpose statement. Second, the titles of the sermon series are reminders of the functions of the church. For example, 'Getting Closer to God' was a series based on the Psalms and was about discipleship, and 'The Wisdom of the Christian Message' was a series with a specific evangelistic application. Third, the regular congregation know the sermon series that are coming and can prepare for them and invite their unchurched friends and neighbours to the ones they think would be the most relevant and appropriate.

The challenge to memorise the purpose statement can come in a number of ways. Interestingly, the children of our church learned the statement because they were practised at memorising Bible verses. We normally give them a certificate to encourage them and to celebrate each verse memorised, so it was no surprise when the tables were turned and the children challenged the adults to memorise the church's purpose statement.

Be imaginative in ways to keep a purpose statement before a church. It is a powerful tool for communicating the vision.

Through faith stories

Faith stories are another way of sharing the vision. If someone is willing to share how they have come to faith or how they have benefited by attending one of the small groups, it serves as a reminder that the vision is working. For example, ask someone to talk about the benefits of attending a ministry group and getting involved in serving others. Ask someone to talk about the benefits of attending the evangelism and mission group and how they feel better equipped to share their faith. Imagine the impact of someone telling how the evangelism and mission group was the vehicle by which God called them to see their workplace in a new light, or even called them into a new area of mission, perhaps overseas.

These steps to share the vision are not to be taken in a particular order, one at a time. You don't first share the sermons and then the purpose statement, and then have small groups followed by faith stories. Initially these steps may begin one at a time, but they build and eventually run simultaneously. That way they gather momentum and make a bigger picture of the vision. For example, faith stories will come from the small groups. The small groups reinforce the vision because they are teaching and implementing the vision. These ideas for sharing vision can run simultaneously and work together, complementing one another, to teach the vision and show it in action.

Through symbols and slogans

Express the vision in a symbol that can soon become familiar to the congregation. There is a church that uses a series of steps to illustrate the journey of both individual Christians and the church, each step representing one of the purposes of the church. This particular church has ten steps representing ten principles, or purposes, on which they are building. Another church uses arrows around a circle, each arrow representing a step forward in the Christian life and the church. Some churches use images that are locally familiar. A church in Denmark uses the four pillars of a bridge, because in southern Denmark bridges are commonplace, linking their many islands together. A church in Essex uses what they call the 'family diamond', combining it with the slogans 'entering the family', 'growing in the family', 'serving in the family', 'extending the family', and 'worshipping as the family'. The Saddleback Church in California uses the baseball diamond, with each base representing a purpose of the church – first base: membership; second base: maturity; third base: ministry; home base: mission; and the pitcher's mound: worship. Our church in Frinton uses a clock face, with each quarter of the clock face representing a purpose and a step forward in the Christian life. We used a clock face because the church has a clock tower with four faces on each side. The clock is a landmark in the community, so the symbol of the clock face connects with both churched and unchurched people.

Use statements and slogans to communicate purpose, balance and vision. For example, our sermon series 'Getting Closer to God' became a slogan we used throughout that series of Sunday messages. The slogan implied action. Another simple slogan we used was 'Praying with Power', which was also the title of a sermon series. Again it called for action.

Make the vision easy for people to understand by using simple statements and symbols.

Through banners

Well-designed banners are a great way to communicate vision. For example, you could have five banners, each one illustrating worshipping, belonging, growing, serving or sharing. Banners enable people to be creative in illustrating the functions and purposes of the church. They highlight the needed balance in church life and at the same time communicate the vision. Some people learn more quickly visually.

Through a church health check

Use a simple church health check. One example, reproduced here with permission, is the Health Check Questionnaire devised by the North Western Baptist Association for all the Baptist churches in that association. They also have two symbols. One is a Purpose Circle, within which are different colours representing different purposes – fellowship, worship, discipleship, outreach, world mission and community. The second symbol is what they describe as a Purpose Enabling Circle. Again, different colours represent the areas that enable the church to fulfil its purposes. In this instance, those areas are vision, leadership, finance and administration, and building.

They have a series of questions to help churches and church members to understand the importance of balance:

1. What do you feel your church is best at?
2. In what area(s) do you feel your church is particularly weak?
3. What do you think the church should be doing/involved in over the next three years?

4. What change do you feel is necessary to make this happen?
5. What gifts/talents are already available to help achieve this goal?
6. What draws you to your church and why do you stay?

A church health check is a great way to help people grasp the principle that there are certain biblical functions that a church should be involved with, and each function needs equal attention.

Through leaders modelling the vision

This is of paramount importance. Leaders, particularly the team leader (vicar, minister, pastor or senior elder), model the vision. Paul, Silas and Timothy wrote to the church in Thessalonica, 'You became a model to all the believers in Macedonia and Achaia' (1 Thessalonians 1:7). People learn best by seeing others live out the vision.

Model the principles needed to make the vision a reality. Live out the principles and purposes in your own life. This will not only communicate the vision, but will also build trust. Leaders set the pace. If you are a true leader, others will follow you. Leaders also recognise and affirm others in the church who are beginning to live out the vision. Encourage your people.

Hopefully you already live a life that is totally committed to Christ and you belong to a local church family. As a leader you will understand the importance of living a life that is growing in Christ; a life of service and sharing, offered to God as an act of lifestyle worship. Leaders must live out the vision in their own lives. They cannot expect a church to catch a vision that they are not willing to live out in their own lives. Leaders embody the values that are needed to accomplish the vision.

Encourage and inspire. Build an understanding of what could be possible in the life of the church and in the lives of its members. Encouragement, inspiration and example go a long way. You must know the vision and have the ability to communicate it clearly. Peter Wagner puts it like this:

> The vision for where God wants the church to go usually is channelled through the pastor. While there are exceptions to this, it has been the case in virtually every study of church growth that I have made. But to be effective, the vision must be communicated to the people in a way that will excite them and motivate them to do their part toward making it a reality. The appropriate channels of communication vary from church to church, but the pulpit is a constant. However, the pulpit is so powerful that you need to make sure the groundwork has been properly laid before announcing your goals. Bulletins and newsletters are constantly used, but there is no substitute for a vision which has gripped the pastor so overwhelmingly that everyone who comes into contact with him or her is bound to catch part of the vision. Visions are caught more than taught.[2]

As stated at the beginning of Chapter 3, a new vision for the local church needs to be grounded in the heart of the leader. The leader must know himself, or herself, in terms of gifting, passions, values, attitudes and experiences. There must be the conviction that God has called them to be the leader of this church for a particular time and a particular reason. Like Esther in Persia, the pastor or vicar is in the church 'for such a time as this' (Esther 4:14). The leader must also know the church and be committed to leading it into the next stage of its journey. Unless the vision, and the commitment to live it out and implement it in the life of the church, is in the heart of the team leader, it simply isn't going to happen.

Having taken the time to get the vision and share it with the leadership and then the rest of the church, now is the time to start the implementation process.

---

[2] C. Peter Wagner, *Leading Your Church to Grow* (Marc Europe, 1986), pp. 194-5.

5

Implementing the Vision

Sometimes the vision is lost because we try to do too many
things at once. A new vision is exciting and motivating, and nat-
urally leaders want to get on with it. But move too quickly, or
try to implement too many changes at once, and it will crash.
Only the leaders can know which is the first step to take. Every
church is different, but there are some principles to follow.

Identify your strengths

Christ says to the church in Sardis, 'Strengthen what remains'
(Revelation 3:2). Wise counsel for a church that is declining.
But also good practical advice for any church that is wanting
to restore balance.

Strengthen what the church is already doing well. As an
example, if the worship is attracting visitors and bringing in
new people from the local community, thank God for it and see
how you can do it better. Seeing in new people should automatically raise the issue of what to do with them. Do they need to
be discipled? Perhaps the church isn't so good at that and discipleship needs to be brought up to speed. What can the church
do to strengthen the weaker areas of church life and begin to
build a better balance? Identifying strengths encourages the

church to move on to the next step. It helps the congregation to recognise possibilities.

Another example may be a church that is very good at social work in the community. As a result it has contact with a lot of people – maybe lots of single-parent families, lonely people, disadvantaged people, people with many different kinds of need. The church buildings might be buzzing with activity, with lots of people on the premises every day of the week. The church may be very innovative in this kind of ministry. Thank God for this and build on it. But how many people are coming to faith and joining the church? The strength of one area of church life often reveals a weakness in another area. Start by building on the strengths rather than the weaknesses. The weaknesses must eventually be addressed, but start by capitalising on the strengths.

The weaknesses are often more quickly identified as the church begins to build on its strengths. As Christian Schwarz reminds us, the shortest stave in a barrel determines the amount of water the barrel can hold. The staves represent the quality characteristics of the church.

Take the next steps in a strategic order

The order of change is different in every church. 'The right plan for change will probably follow the purpose, target and strategy order. Changes in purpose should be made first. Changes in target should be made next. Changes in strategy – which are the most visible changes – should be made last.'[1]

Purpose

Your purpose is a good place to begin. The purpose statement is reminding the church of why it exists. Hopefully this has been worked through during the vision-building process. It makes

---

[1] Dan Southerland, *Transitioning* (Zondervan, 2000), pp. 101–102.

sense therefore to start with your purpose, even if the actual statement has not yet been written down.

At Frinton Free Church we began with our purpose. The purpose statement wasn't fully developed at that time, but the purpose of the church was clear. Even when your statement has been written down it will probably take time to fine-tune it. Some churches have a number of revisions of their actual purpose statement, but their purpose is nevertheless clear. The purpose statement of the church in Frinton is:

To help people become fully developed followers of Jesus Christ, enable them to worship God together and equip them for ministry in the church and mission in the world.

- 'Followers of Jesus Christ' means we must engage in mission and evangelism.
- 'Fully developed followers of Jesus Christ' means we must disciple them.
- 'Enable them to worship God' means teaching them that worship is a lifestyle.
- 'Enable them to worship God together' means bringing them into the body of Christ, the family of God, the church.
- 'Equip them for ministry in the church' means providing mentoring, training and accountability.
- 'And mission in the world' means further training and equipping for mission in the community and beyond.

Notice how our purpose statement spells out exactly what we believe God wants us to do – how he wants his church to function. The statement implies balance, and at the same time helps us to review whether or not we are achieving our purposes. Beware of being too idealistic. Remember there is no such thing as a perfectly balanced church. We should, however, try and avoid division: 'Make every effort to keep the unity of the Spirit' (Ephesians 4:3).

As the church began to makes changes in line with its purpose, and as we focused on helping people to become 'followers of Jesus Christ', we began to make changes to our worship services. We also increased the number of our worship services to include two morning services, an afternoon traditional service for older folk or those who would prefer a more traditional approach, and two evening services. One was entirely for youth. We wanted to make our Sunday services attractive and relevant to the unchurched. The church became more seeker-sensitive. The preaching was one of the easiest things to change. The church became more proactive in welcoming visitors. The regular congregation became more confident in inviting friends and neighbours. Those attending the weekday activities, many of which were designed as outreach, were encouraged to make the big step of attending church on Sundays. This reminded us that we had only one opportunity to make a first impression. This further focused our attention on making the worship welcoming, attractive and relevant.

Targeting

The church became more intentional about targeting the community. Special non-threatening outreach events were arranged, including showing live World Cup football on the church's large screen. Part of the targeting strategy was to raise community confidence in the church, to help people see that it was a 'safe' place to visit. After one such event the following headline appeared in the local paper: 'Church night out a great experience.' Underneath the headline was this letter:

> As a new resident in Frinton, I took up the invitation from the Frinton Free Church organisers to attend the screening of the Germany versus England football match on the church premises on Saturday night.
>
> My three grandsons, who are ardent football fans, also came with me. To say that we enjoyed the experience would be an understatement and while some of the pleasure was no doubt due to the

final score, it was mainly down to the way we were welcomed into the church and made to feel totally at home by the organisers, as I am sure were all of the other 50 to 60 (or even more) people present.

The atmosphere and presentation was excellent. I would like to thank the organisers for this innovative presentation and for making us all so welcome.

It will certainly be an evening well remembered.

Talk about free advertising! The letter also reaffirmed that implementing our vision was working. Other events targeting the community were organised: visits from the African Children's Choir, sports weekends and visits from well-known Christian celebrities with something to say. The church already ran the well-known Alpha courses, now incorporated as part of our targeting strategy.

One of the most significant pieces of targeting was to help newcomers into another small group besides Alpha. The church had not always been successful at keeping newcomers, so there was a need to set up a 'way in' to the church family. By starting a group for newcomers, we were also building the church from the outside in. Most of us have been taught to build from the inside out, but newcomers grasp the vision quickly. They have far less luggage from the past, if any. So without neglecting existing church members, we focus very much on new people.

Existing church members can 'sit in' on the newcomers' group if there is space. Although there are other teaching groups for them, they are also encouraged to attend a 'Newcomers for Oldcomers' teaching time. This takes place on a Sunday afternoon following lunch together and helps them to be aware of how newcomers are incorporated into the church family. Some churches take all their existing members through such a group so that everyone knows how the church reaches out to new people.

The newcomers' group meets one evening a week in the

senior minister's home for approximately eight weeks, and finishes with a meal. People are often curious to see how the vicar lives and it also gives the minister the advantage of getting to know the new people. It gives the newcomers the opportunity to ask questions and find out more about what it means to be a Christian and to be part of a local church. If I were starting a new church or was in a very small church, I would still invite new people into our home, even if it was only one or two.

Strategy

The church was now beginning to build a strategy in order to fulfil its purpose. We asked what the church needed to do 'to help people become fully developed followers of Jesus Christ, enable them to worship God together and equip them for ministry in the church and mission in the world'. As the church began to implement the purpose and target the community, it needed to develop a strategy to follow through. It needed to take practical steps to bring people into the church family, and equip them for ministry and mission. We therefore developed a four-step process by learning from Saddleback Church in California, in which we focused on newcomers, maturity, ministry and mission.

Saddleback Church is built on a five-step strategy that attracts and wins the unchurched, develops them to spiritual maturity, equips them for a ministry, and then helps them establish a life mission in the world. A simple baseball diamond is used as a visual road map to help people understand their journey with God. Each base in the diamond represents a point of growth. The first base is a class on church *membership*, calling for a commitment to Saddleback's membership covenant. The second base is a class leading up to making a commitment to a *spiritual growth* covenant. Third base is a *ministry* class leading to a commitment to serve in the ministry of the church. Members then move back to the home plate by completing a class on *mission* and making a commitment to sharing their faith in the community and workplace and on mission trips. The fifth step in the overall strategy is to learn how to celebrate God's presence through *worship*. We will look at the fifth step in Chapter 7.

Frinton Free Church developed a very similar strategy for helping unchurched people to become mature believers who fulfil their ministry in the church and mission in the world. From beginning with just the newcomers' group the church developed a strategy that has grown and grown, touching every part of the church's life, teaching the importance of living a balanced Christian life around the purposes of God, and thereby building balance into the church overall.

1. *Membership.*   From the first moment a visitor from the local community steps onto the premises a journey begins, which, unless they choose to opt out, will continue for the rest of the time they are part of the church family.

Over a period of five years the newcomers' group welcomed over 300 visitors, of which over 200 made the commitment to church membership. For some there were intermediate steps, such as attending Alpha or another of our seeker groups. In an informal home environment, the newcomers' group covers biblical teaching about being a Christian and the importance of belonging to a local church family. The subjects of baptism and communion are also discussed. One whole session is about our particular church – its history, how it is structured, and why it does things the way it does. The strategy for mission is explained, along with how the worship services are planned and what we believe to be our purposes. Newcomers are asked to reflect on whether this church is the one for them. Sometimes people who have been members of churches in other parts of the country, particularly another Baptist church, assume that this church is just like the one they left. That means they could join the church with a false set of expectations and then become frustrated. We welcome the experiences and gifts that new people bring into the church. Until we ran this group we were actually losing visitors because we were not helping them to find their way in.

Newcomers are first made aware of this opportunity in a number of ways. A simple get-together one Sunday afternoon is arranged for those who have recently started to attend the church. At that time they are given information about the newcomers' house group. The first step is Sunday afternoon. The second step is to join the group.

The church is intentional about identifying newcomers on Sundays and during the week. Unless that itself is a strategy, the connection may not be made. Personal invitations are given by telephone and letter. This takes effort, but the personal contact is vital and is best organised by a small, dedicated team.

It's not long before newcomers begin to have an effect on the church. They are often some of the most enthusiastic and willing workers. They grasp the vision quickly. After a few months they start helping to welcome other new people. They are the best people to do that because they are so positive about their own experience, and they know how important a warm welcome is.

We have found that having 200 new church members in five years makes an impact on a church. As the church reaches more and more unchurched, the worship services have to be adapted to accommodate them, so changes have to be implemented in the area of corporate worship. Knowledge of the Bible, for example, cannot be taken for granted. Neither can it be assumed that the language of the Christian church will be immediately understood.

Each implementation of the vision has a knock-on effect. From the newcomers' group people have a number of options. They may choose to go to an Alpha group to learn Christian basics (unless of course they have come from an Alpha group), attend a baptism class or discipleship group, or they may be ready for church membership and choose to join a permanent home Bible study group.

Implementing the vision step by step is an exciting process. Focusing on the purpose helps to strategise. As the church begins to work from the outside in, working at reaching new people, the strategy almost automatically begins to unfold. What does the church do next to help people continue their journey? Sometimes, perhaps more often than we like to think, churches welcome new members, but they are then expected to fend for themselves. I have often heard people say, 'Once I joined the church, everything seemed to stop.' As though joining the church was the ultimate goal. This is only the beginning of the journey. If you want to build a biblically balanced church, you must go further.

2. *Spiritual growth.*   At Frinton, the next stage in the strategy is to provide a spiritual growth group. This is another weekly home group that meets for eight weeks, and it is called Maturity Matters. It is adaptable for people at various stages of spiritual growth and is suitable for people who have made a commitment and come to faith in Christ through an Alpha course. It has also proved to be helpful to people who have been Christians for many years, since the road to Christian maturity is a life-long journey. Spiritual maturity is a constant theme in the apostle Paul's letters to the churches. Concerning his own journey he says to the church at Philippi:

> Not that I have . . . already been made perfect, but I press on to take hold of that for which Christ Jesus took hold of me . . . Forgetting what is behind and straining towards what is ahead, I press on towards the goal to win the prize for which God has called me heavenwards in Christ Jesus. All of us who are mature should take such a view of things. (Philippians 3:12–15)

This group covers practical ways of studying and applying the Bible, building a deepening relationship with God, maintaining an effective prayer life and learning how to relate to others as members of the body of Christ, and it looks at how giving is part of the believer's relationship with Christ and the church. Although these are basic elements of the Christian life, every Christian can grow in each of these areas. Older as well as newer Christians have enthusiastically attended this course. Knowing that it lasts for a specified period of eight weeks has an attraction. It is a long enough period of time for people to bond and most groups are reluctant to end.

Along with other specialist groups it is set in the context of our normal weekly home groups. Some people have opted out of their home groups for the course, and some people have been encouraged to join a regular home group, having been part of this one. This course, along with the newcomers' house group, Alpha and other special groups, runs three times a year, and hundreds of church members have benefited.

The practical material not only provides knowledge, or confirms knowledge people already have, but provides them with the tools to apply it. It is this 'how to do it' approach that has been welcomed. It demonstrates that what has been missing in many churches is teaching about the application of belief to the Christian life. People welcome being shown how to grow as a Christian, how to go about Bible study, prayer, giving and belonging to the church family. In many churches it is taken for granted that newcomers will know this. This is part of the strategy 'to help people become fully developed followers of Jesus Christ'.

3. *Ministry*. 'To equip them for ministry' requires another intentional process. It doesn't happen automatically. So a third home group called Ministry Matters was set up. Throughout the course we use the acronym SHAPE. This was developed years ago by Rick Warren to explain the five elements that determine a person's ministry.

- S stands for *spiritual gifts*. Teaching what the Bible has to say about gifting, members of the group are encouraged to reflect on what gift they may have. At this point they can use a carefully prepared questionnaire. Members are also encouraged to interact with one another and reflect on what others may have observed about their giftedness. This is only the first step in the process of discovering how God has 'shaped' us.

  Many churches find themselves need-driven rather than gift-driven. They have a long list of jobs to be done and they spend their time looking for anyone who can fill those vacancies, regardless of gifting. A lot of energy and time are spent trying to find people simply to do the work that needs to be done. That same energy and time could be used in developing a strategy for becoming a church that uses the gifts of its members to determine its ministries. This will also help to prevent people becoming square pegs in round holes. This part of the strategy helps to break out of the vicious circle of being need-driven so that the church can unleash its potential. Discovering the gifting of the membership guides the church to decide what ministries it should have.

- H stands for *heart*. Christians talk about having a heart for children, for the elderly or for some group of people for whom they have a special concern. Some Christians talk about having a heart for a particular country, for a particular race of people or for an area of the church's ministry. Members of the group are asked, 'Who or what do you think God has given you a heart for?' Jesus said, 'For out of the overflow of the heart the mouth speaks' (Matthew 12:34). The heart represents what we feel passionate about. It is a valid guide to where God wants us to serve.

- A stands for *abilities*. Everybody has a set of abilities that they have probably been using for years in many different areas of life. They may have become used to them and take them for granted and think them unimportant. Yet they are natural abilities and skills that God wants to use and develop. Some abilities may become gifts. Members are asked to reflect on how God has used them in their past, or what things they have been good at, even before they became a Christian.

- P stands for *personality*, or temperament. God has made us all different. Some people are introverts and some are extroverts. Some people love routine; others prefer the freedom of spontaneity. An awareness of our temperament is important, as it will determine the way in which our gift will be used. An introvert will use the gift of encouragement in a very different way from an extrovert. The goal here is to help people towards self-awareness of their own personality, to reflect on how God may use their giftedness.

- E stands for life *experiences*. Over the years people will have passed through many different experiences, some painful. Out of these experiences may come a ministry. Paul writes to the Christians in Corinth about, 'the God of all comfort, who comforts us in all our troubles, so that we can comfort those in any trouble with the comfort we ourselves have received from God' (2 Corinthians 1:3–4). God wants to use the experiences we have been through. I am deeply impressed and helped by something Bishop Phillips Brooks wrote over a hundred years ago:

> Every new experience is a new opportunity of knowing God. Every new experience is like a jewel set into the texture of our life, on which God shines and makes interpretation and revelation of himself. He wastes nothing. There are some who want to get away from their past. Their life with Christ seems one long failure. But you must learn, you must let God teach you. That the only way to get rid of your past is to get a future out of it. God will waste nothing. There is something in your past, something, even if it only be the sin of which you have repented, which, if you can put it into the Saviour's hands, will be a new life for you.[2]

---

[2] Phillips Brooks, *Phillips Brooks Year Book* (Macmillan, 1903).

Exploring these five aspects of development helps each member to understand their SHAPE – the ministry that God has shaped them for. It is not just giftedness that determines ministry. It is the total person. Rick Warren says, 'You will be most effective and fulfilled in ministry when you use your *spiritual gifts* and *abilities* in the area of your *heart's* desire in a way that best expresses your *personality* and *experiences*.' (If you are interested to discover more about SHAPE, read *The Purpose Driven Church*.)

We have discovered that this approach to helping people into the ministry of the local church has motivated them to get involved. It awakens them to the realisation that they do have something to offer. It also helps them to achieve a better balance between the responsibilities of work, home and church. Some of our members have been more motivated to see their work as a place of ministry as well as taking some responsibility in church.

But the course is only the beginning. After a one-to-one placement interview we work to find an outlet for each person's ministry. The course will affirm for some that they are already serving where God wants them to serve. For others it will mean a change of direction or taking up a new responsibility. We try to match a person's SHAPE to a ministry that already exists in the church. If there isn't one, we might start a new ministry. Instead of having only a list of vacancies, we also build a list of people ready to serve. It has been thrilling to see the impact of this course on the lives of many individual members and the church as a whole. This is an area where a lot of potential has been released.

With some people there needs to be a period of training. It is vital that people in ministry are nurtured, equipped, supported and know who they are accountable to. It is not only emotional and spiritual support that is needed, but also practical support, such as access to office supplies and equipment, teaching materials and anything that enables them to carry out their ministry.

Equipping and setting people free for ministry is part of a strategy for growth. This is the kind of thing we see in Acts 6. We have already seen that when the apostles took steps to ensure that certain widows were no longer overlooked 'in the daily distribution of food', they also removed what would have become a hindrance to the continuing growth of the church. The apostles looked for others who could be appointed to this practical ministry while they continued to exercise 'the ministry of the word': 'We will turn this responsibility over to them and will give our attention to prayer and the ministry of the word' (Acts 6:3–4). The result was that 'the word of God spread. The number of disciples in Jerusalem increased rapidly, and a large number of priests became obedient to the faith' (Acts 6:7).

This approach to equipping people resulted in us appointing a full-time ministry pastor in 2003. The church has frequently been asked for the job description of this post, so an outline has been included at the end of this chapter.

4. *Mission.*   'Mission in the world.' The vision is to send fully devoted followers of Jesus Christ back out into the world, so that their journey can be repeated by others. So another eight-week home group was set up called Mission Matters. The teaching in this group aims to help people share their faith with friends, neighbours and work colleagues. The teaching also includes getting a view on what God is doing in the wider world. It is possible that from this group will come future vocational missionaries.

These groups are just one example of how the implementation process can happen. Having established under God the vision for the church, follow the purpose of that vision and build the strategy to achieve the purpose. None of this happens quickly. Our groups did not all happen at once. It was a process that took two years. The first group, Newcomers, was set up. The material was prepared and people were invited. It was taught by the senior pastor, with a future leader sitting in on it. Next the discipleship group, Maturity Matters, was set up – again initially taught by the senior pastor with someone else sitting in, learning the material. Then came the third group, Ministry Matters, followed by the fourth group, Mission Matters.

Once the strategy is in place and working, the whole process speeds up. This is the exciting part. As each of the four groups is taught three or four times a year, people are growing, getting involved in ministry and mission, gaining confidence to share their faith, bringing others along to the church. It becomes growth on growth.

Gradually the vision unfolds. Some people find it difficult to visualise, but those who find the vision difficult to see in the beginning, see it later as it begins to happen. The most visible change in church life is strategy, and this happens last in the implementation process. It can happen in almost any size church, in any cultural setting, as a later chapter will show.

But this is only the beginning!

MINISTRY PASTOR JOB DESCRIPTION

Vision

- To release members into their potential for ministry.

Purpose

- To build and develop the biblical principles of every member ministry in the life of Frinton Free Church.
- To oversee the teaching of the Ministry Matters group, giving particular attention to the reflection process included in the SHAPE concept.
- To continually evaluate and adapt the group material to the needs of Frinton Free members.

- To inspire and motivate church members to attend Ministry Matters.
- To be responsible for the placing of church members within the various ministry teams of the church.
- To oversee a mentoring and training process.
- To be responsible for setting up new ministries as prompted by the discovery of new ministry gifts in the lives of individual church members.

Accountability

- The ministry leader will be a member of the pastoral team and responsible to the senior pastor.

Requirements

- A mature Christian with good relationship skills, able to inspire and encourage individuals towards discovering and implementing God's purpose for their lives.
- An understanding of the biblical principles of every-member ministry.
- A willingness to spend time with people in a mentoring process.
- Previous experience in ministry and basic theological and biblical studies.

General

- Further training and opportunities to develop as the ministry leader will be offered and encouraged.

6

Structuring the Church to Serve its Purpose

The reason why some churches remain small is because they are structured that way. Create structures that will provide room for the church to grow. Some churches may not realise it, but their current structures are barriers to growth. And some structures are deeply rooted in the life of the church. Outdated structures restrict the creativity of the congregation. A good structure will allow the church to change and grow. A bad structure will restrict the health and growth of a church. A good structure will support and facilitate the purposes and mission of the church, enabling it to be balanced and healthy. Think of the structure serving the same function as the skeleton does in the human body.

A church's structure can either serve the church or bring it to a standstill. It can energize a community of faith or lead it towards ever deepening levels of discouragement. It can enable men and women to use their gifts and abilities for the kingdom of God or tie the hands and frustrate the most dedicated efforts of God's people. Why? Because the structure of any organization directly affects morale, effectiveness, and unity.[1]

---

[1] James Emery White, *Rethinking the Church* (Baker Books, 1997), p. 94.

Structure for growth, not control

'Every church must eventually decide whether it will be structured for *control* or structured for *growth*.'[2] There are too many churches where people are serving the structure rather than the structure enabling the people to grow and be involved in ministry and mission. Sometimes PCCs, elders, deacons and even pastors are viewed as policing bodies. Every detailed decision has to be passed by them. This eventually has a discouraging effect on the membership. Healthy, growing churches think less about structures and more about ministry. They emphasise flexibility, simplicity, relationships and functionality.

Some churches do not realise they are structured for control. In such churches it has always been assumed that the PCC or deacons, or other board, will vet every decision and action. It's never been done any other way. The congregation may be comfortable with this because it relieves them of responsibility and involvement. And the governing council think this is the way it is supposed to be, and in many instances quite like the control. Some people enjoy the power and status of such governing bodies. But if a church is structured for control it will eventually stifle the creativity of its members, restrict the growth of the church and create a lot of frustration. This kind of structure also sets the church up for lots of meetings.

To give up control is not easy. Current members of bodies such as the PCC may not like it. They may feel threatened. They may dislike the feeling of being out of control. Some education is therefore necessary if the church is to be structured for growth, and for a lot of churches this will involve a change of mindset. It also calls for a step of faith. It feels risky to let go of control. This doesn't mean there is no accountability. It's just that accountability is handled in a different way, as explained later in this chapter. But being structured for growth sets people

---

[2] Rick Warren, *The Purpose Driven Church* (Zondervan, 1995), p. 378.

free for ministry. It sets them free from meetings and committees so they have more time for ministry. 'Most churches are not structured for the laity to do ministry. Persons involved in the church often spend their time on committees or boards rather than in front-line ministry.'[3]

Structuring for growth is a major step for some churches, partly because in some mainstream denominations structures are imposed from outside. Such structures can militate against the purposes, balance and health of the local church. In these instances, the church may be obliged to work within those limitations. Whatever form of government a church is under – Church of England, Salvation Army, Methodist, Baptist, whether episcopal or congregational – structures can restrict or encourage growth. In most local churches, however, there is room to change. Don't immediately try to remove old methods and structures. Place the new structures alongside the older ones and watch the older structures begin to be ineffective. In some instances the new structures may actually work alongside the old structures to the point where they complement each other.

Here are some suggestions for taking your church forward to being a fully functioning biblical church that is balanced in its life and work.

Structure around your purposes

If the purposes of the church are worship, fellowship and pastoral care, discipleship, evangelism and ministry, structure around those purposes. For example, place all the discipleship activities of the church under the heading of 'discipleship', or whatever title you choose. Appoint a leader to head up a discipleship team. The leader appointed does *not* have to be a clergy person, a member of the PCC, a deacon or an elder. However,

---

[3] Thom Rainer, *The Book of Church Growth* (Broadman, 1993), p. 200.

the team leader will ultimately be accountable to the governing body of the church, whatever that may be. But the governing body sets that leader free to head up that particular ministry. This is letting go of the ministry. What is different here is that most churches want to keep a leader with this amount of responsibility as part of the PCC or board of deacons.

Appoint a leader for each of the functions or purposes of the church – as many leaders as the church has purposes. Hopefully the church has simplified its purposes so that the new structure is not too complex. At Frinton Free Church we appointed five purpose leaders, one for each purpose the church has identified. Each leader has a team. Members of the team are accountable to the team leader, and the team leaders are accountable to the elders.

The church has to decide which activities and ministries come under which purpose. One way to do this is to decide the primary purpose of each activity. Each activity or ministry in the local church will have a primary purpose and a secondary or even third purpose. For example, if a church runs an Internet café, it must decide the primary purpose of that ministry. Is it outreach? Is it fellowship? Is it discipleship? It may decide that the primary purpose is outreach – mission. The secondary purpose might be seen as fellowship, creating a sense of belonging. Deciding what is the primary purpose of a church activity focuses the effectiveness of that ministry, makes decision-making easier, and helps leader and team members to clarify their roles.

Work through all the activities of the church and place each one under one of the purposes of the church, according to the vision of the church. Again, this is not something to be done in a hurry. Take time over it. It's a process. Some churches have tried to achieve restructuring all at once and have caused confusion. The best way to do this is to work with people and not committees. Help people involved in the activities of the church to work out for themselves the primary purpose of what they do. It is always better if they own their sense of purpose rather than being told what it is. Of course, church leaders will want to give guidance and suggestions, but the purpose is owned by those who are directly involved in that particular ministry.

It is unlikely that the average church will find all of its purpose team leaders at one time. In some smaller churches, one person may need to lead two teams of workers. It is not necessary to identify all five (or however many leaders you want) at one time. Choose them carefully over a period of time. Allow this new structure of church life to grow gradually. It may take five years to find your leaders, but don't give up.

Have a goal for the restructuring of your church

If you are in a 50-member church, imagine what kind of structure you will need if it grows to be a 100-member church, and then structure it that way. If you are in a 150-member church, imagine what kind of structure you will need if it doubles in size, then build a structure for a 300-member church. If you are in a 300-member church, structure it as a 600-member church. In this way, rather than growing out of an old structure, the church grows into the new structure gradually.

Structuring around the purposes of your church doesn't mean starting with the proverbial clean sheet of paper. Being radical doesn't mean sweeping away the old and bringing in the new. What it does mean is starting out on a journey that may take a long time, but has a definite goal in view.

Here is a quick summary of what this structure may look like. There is a team of overall leaders, which may include full-time clergy (ministers, pastors) and volunteer leaders (deacons, elders, church wardens). Next there is the team of purpose leaders, which may be quite different people, or include some members of the overall leadership team. The purpose leaders oversee their respective teams (worship, membership, disciple-ship, ministry and mission). There is accountability within the overall leadership and purpose-leaders groups. Ultimately, if you have five purposes in your church, the activities are run by workers who belong to the purpose team for that activity. This means that the leader of each organisation in the church knows to whom they are accountable and from whom they can expect support.

The five purposes interact with each other across the whole church. They do not work in isolation from each other, but more like warp and weft in a piece of cloth. For example, someone working in a weekday coffee shop may be in an activity that comes under the mission purpose of the church. The individual concerned may have a heart for mission, and the coffee shop is where they most see their gifts and experience at work. However, although the coffee shop team is accountable to the mission leader, each individual is exercising their ministry and therefore seeks training and mentoring from the ministry team. The coffee shop team also needs to liaise with the fellowship team leader, as fellowship may be a strong secondary ministry in the coffee shop.

In churches that have both elders and deacons the question is often asked, 'What is the role of the deacons in this kind of structure?' The deacons' responsibility is to provide the practical tools – finance, buildings, office, equipment, etc. – to enable each team to function. When people are appointed to a ministry they need to have the resources to carry out that ministry. As well as the church office, the Frinton church was able to have another room with a desk and computer terminal that could be booked by the various team leaders in the church.

Rainer quotes Carl George, Director of the Charles E. Fuller Institute of Evangelism and Church Growth in California: 'Have a change of mind about how ministry is to be done and a change of form in the infrastructure of the church.'[4]

---

[4] Thom Rainer, *The Book of Church Growth* (Broadman, 1993), p. 296.

Structure around people

Too many churches are structured around committees, policies and rules. The aim of structuring around purposes and people is to build a sense of community. Bill Gates, Chairman of Microsoft, says, 'Individuals generate ideas, and Microsoft makes it possible for those ideas to become a reality.'[5] The aim of church leadership is to make it possible for individuals to fulfil their ministry.

The church is a family. It is not a club or an organisation. It is a body – the body of Christ. The local church is a family of believers who are at different levels of spiritual maturity. Each individual is on a journey with God and a journey that needs to be recognised and respected. As well as encouraging and motivating members to be involved in ministry, it also needs to be recognised that these same members are in the church to be cared for, pastored and ministered to. By building around people we implement strong biblical principles: 'Just as each of us has one body with many members, and these members do not all have the same function, so in Christ we who are many form one body, and each member belongs to all the others' (Romans 12:4–5). The apostle Paul goes on to say:

> We have different gifts, according to the grace given us. If a man's gift is prophesying, let him use it in proportion to his faith. If it is serving, let him serve; if it is teaching, let him teach; if it is encouraging, let him encourage; if it is contributing to the needs of others, let him give generously; if it is leadership, let him govern diligently; if it is showing mercy, let him do it cheerfully. (Romans 12:6–8)

> From him the whole body, joined and held together by every supporting ligament, grows and builds itself up in love, as each part does its work. (Ephesians 4:16)

---

[5] James Emery White, *Rethinking the Church* (Baker Books, 1997), p. 96.

In George Barna's *User-Friendly Churches*, he explains that successful churches 'subscribe to a common philosophy: the ministry is not called to fit the church's structure; the structure exists to further effective ministry'. That means that when the structure doesn't work, it is changed. Barna adds:

> These churches had a keen sense of direction and purpose (i.e. vision and plans). *Their top priority was to achieve their ministry goals.* If the organisational charts and structural procedures inhibited such ministry, they would cautiously but willingly work around the barriers. They were not about to let a man-made system hinder their ability to take advantage of a God-given opportunity to change lives for the Kingdom. Structure, in fact, was not an issue in these churches. Certainly, these congregations were led by individuals who see the wisdom of developing and maintaining orderly processes. They recognised the importance of formal hierarchy of authority, and the importance of avoiding anarchy (even if the intentions of the anarchists are good). *But structure was viewed as a support system, a means to an end, rather than an end in itself.* The structures they used had been developed, accepted, implemented, re-evaluated and upgraded. At all times, the focus was upon ministry, not structure.[6] (Italics mine)

Structure around teams

When Nehemiah was rebuilding the walls of Jerusalem he organised the people to work in teams. The difference between teams and committees is that teams do the work of ministry while committees tend to be discussing ministry. If we had a cleaning committee, the committee would discuss how the work of cleaning the premises should be done. If we had a cleaning team, they would be the people who do the cleaning. As a team they may have discussion while on the job, and some

---

[6] Leith Anderson (quoting Barna), *A Church For The 21st Century* (Bethany House, 1992), p. 139.

decisions will be made, but they will be made by the people actually doing the work, and that is the crucial difference between a team of workers and a committee of people telling workers what to do.

Teams also tend to focus on ministry rather than maintenance, and one of the aims of restructuring is to move the church from a maintenance mindset to a ministry mindset. Building around teams focuses people as ministers, rather than the clergy being seen as ministers, and it helps members to focus on the purposes of the church.

Being in a team provides an opportunity for fellowship. Being in a team is one of the quickest ways to learn and to grow spiritually. Being in a team is, of course, all about serving God by serving others. Being in a team helps people to focus on the overall purpose of the church; namely to reach others in the community for Christ. And being in a team is about offering our lives to God as an act of worship. So all five purposes are involved in being part of a team.

Appointing people to teams rather than committees is a new paradigm. William Eason, in *Sacred Cows Make Gourmet Burgers: Ministry Anytime, Anywhere, by Anybody*, says that effective churches 'believe that the role of God's people is to minister to people, in the world, every day of the week, by living out their spiritual gifts instead of running the church by sitting on committees and making decisions about what can or cannot be done'.[7]

These are some of the teams at Frinton Free Church:

Catering Teams	Weekday Crèche Team
Sound System Team	Audio Visual Team
Reception Team for our	Ladies' Ministry Team
drop in centre	Parents and Toddlers Team

---

[7] William Eason, *Sacred Cows Make Gourmet Burgers: Ministry Anytime, Anywhere, by Anybody* (Abingdon, 1995), p. 55.

Cleaning Team
Communion Preparation
  Team
Youth Team
Children's Team
Sports Ministry Team
Stewards' Team
Prayer Teams
Finance Team
Church Office Team
Bereavement Support Group
  Team
Music and Worship Teams
Art Workshop Team
Flower Ministry Team

Coffee Pot Team (our coffee
  shop)
Bible Group Leaders' Team
  (house groups)
Missionaries' Support Teams
Pastoral Carers' Team
Banner-Making Team
Alpha Group Team
Newcomers' Team
Maturity Matters Team
Mission Matters Team
Mission Team
Ministry Matters Team
Information Table Team
  (Sundays)
Welcomers' Team

These are not in any order of priority. They simply show how people are working and serving and exercising ministry together in ministry teams. The teams represent many ministries in the church, and there are teams within teams. Building around teams enables people to own the ministry. They feel trusted. As mentioned, each of these teams belongs to one of the five purpose teams. Even if a particular task requires only one person, it is supportive for that person if they belong to a wider team.

Every now and again it is helpful to remind the entire church of the various teams that are ministering in the church. On one Sunday in April 2003, the members of Frinton Free Church held what was called a ministry fair. The halls and rooms of the church were turned into a local church resources exhibition. Each team in the church was asked to provide a stand displaying their ministry. There were 40 'stands'. Established church members were surprised at how many ministries there were in their own church.

Exhibiting local church ministries in this way makes several powerful points. First, the visual impact on the church is far greater than simply listing various ministries of the church in a weekly bulletin, or giving reports at church meetings. The ministry teams received huge encouragement from church members who discovered more fully what the different teams in the church were about. Everybody across the whole church, including those who were already committed to the church and involved in a ministry, was surprised and encouraged by the range of ministries. The visual impact was strikingly effective.

Second, the day proved to be a useful recruiting ground for drawing new people, or people who were not involved in a ministry, into a ministry team. They were able to look at the range of ministries in the church, collect a lot more information about each ministry than they could normally do, ask as many questions as they liked, and decide where they believed they could best serve. Over 70 people joined a ministry. For many months we had asked for more people to help prepare the communion table, but no one had volunteered. In the ministry fair, one of the stands simply showed what was involved in serving communion. This caught the imagination of some people, who then happily volunteered to help.

A third benefit was an opportunity for the local community to get an idea of what church is about. People from outside were easily made aware that the local church was far more than a place where people came to sing hymns on Sundays. The day exploded a lot of myths about what a local Christian church is all about. Other churches around the UK have organised similar fairs with great benefits to both the church and the community.

Structure around small groups

Structuring around small groups is also a key to church health and growth. Chapter 8 deals with small groups in greater depth, but notice here their place in the structure of the local church, particularly a larger church. Some teams may themselves be a small group: 'A ministry team is nothing more than a small group of people with a complementary assortment of gifts and abilities who are committed to a particular ministry that supports the ministry and mission of the church.'[8]

Small groups are places not only for fellowship, teaching and the other purposes of the church, but also for sharing and owning vision. Small group leaders are key leaders of the church, serving as lay pastors. Together they form a team which comes under the care of the discipleship leader.

Keep the structure simple

Some church structures, even in very small churches, are exceedingly complex. They become bureaucratic and, as a consequence, inhibiting. One of the advantages of building a balanced church is that it provides the opportunity for a clear and simplified structure. The structure needs to be reviewed at least once a year to make sure that it is actually serving the purposes of the church. It is so easy for any structure, committee or policy to become an end in itself. People then end up serving the structure. How things are done can become more important than what is done. Never allow structure to become more important than function. Remember that Jesus said, 'The Sabbath was made to benefit people, and not people to benefit the Sabbath' (Mark 2:27, NLT).

Rick Warren says, 'Streamline your structure to maximize ministry and minimize maintenance.'[9] Teach people the difference between maintenance and ministry. Ministry is what the people do and maintenance, the running of the church, is done by the leaders or paid staff. Warren also points out that 'a common mistake made by many churches is to take their

---

[8] James Emery White, *Rethinking the Church* (Baker Books, 1997), p. 102.
[9] Rick Warren, *The Purpose Driven Church* (Zondervan, 1995), p. 379.

brightest and best people and turn them into bureaucrats by giving them more meetings to attend. You can drain the life out of people by scheduling a constant string of committee meetings.'[10]

The risk factor

This kind of church structure involves trust. And trust always includes risk. Turning the ministry of the church over to the people, to what used to be called the laity, is a risk. They will make mistakes, but without making mistakes they will never learn. Trying to run a church without making any mistakes is impossible. We can become so anxious to make sure everything is done properly that we slowly strangle the effectiveness of the church. As mentioned at the beginning of this chapter, the choice is between structuring for control or structuring for growth. Control may reduce the possibility of mistakes, but it will also reduce the possibility of growth.

Structuring for growth will call for the leadership to trust the membership and the membership to trust the leadership. How many churches are prepared for this level of trust? It is the only way forward when a church reaches about 500 people, for at this stage the church will only grow when the leadership team realises that no one member can possibly know everything that is going on in the church any more. If, as a church member, you are prepared to trust your leaders, even when they make mistakes, provided they are genuinely seeking God's purposes, and if as a leader you are prepared to trust them with the ministry of your church, then you can move on to the next step of becoming a balanced, healthy, growing church.

---

[10] Rick Warren, *The Purpose Driven Church* (Zondervan, 1995), p. 376.

7

Imagine Your Church Achieving its Mission

Imagine a church that is winning the confidence of the community. A church that is meeting community needs. A church where the worship is touching the lives of new people every week. A church that people can't wait to come to.

Imagine a church where bruised, addicted, lonely, depressed and anxious people find hope and a purpose for their lives, and start to reach out to others. A church where people regularly come to faith in Christ and begin to grow as disciples.

Imagine a church where people can't wait to get involved in the ministries of the church and to share their new-found faith with work friends, family and social contacts.

Imagine a church where people find worship so inspiring and relevant they can't wait to come back. A church where new believers learn how to grow spiritually and begin to live by biblical principles and values. Imagine.

As Joel Edwards of the UK Evangelical Alliance said:

Imagine a Church that refuses to settle for the way things are. What might it be like to belong to a Church whose primary preoccupation was not fulfilling internal agendas but meeting its mission to make Jesus known and loved in a real world? A Church concerned not just about getting more people inside the building, but turning out contemporary disciples – disciples equipped to love and serve the world, and see other people come to faith in Christ? A Church called to do more than survive, but energised to escape the gravitational pull of secondary matters that keep us from our primary purpose.[1]

Let's have a look at what might be possible.

Worship

If the strategy of the church is to make disciples, the content of the worship services may need to be reviewed: 'The worshipping life of most churches is largely built on two assumptions that are seldom verbalised yet are highly influential. The first is that worship should be traditional in its expression, and second, that it is an event solely for the believer and, as a result, is irrelevant to non-Christians.'[2] These two assumptions have taken a painful toll on many UK churches, resulting in decades of decline in church attendance.

For many people, 'church' means 'dull, boring and irrelevant'. A few years ago a book came out called *101 Things to Do with a Dull Church*.[3] It's a great book and fun to read, but the fact that it exists speaks volumes! What the book is saying is that the church has a reputation for irrelevance and boredom.

Worship is an emotionally sensitive issue for many Christians, because we have personal preferences that are often a reflection of our own personalities and traditions. It is difficult to set our preferences aside, and the only way we can do that is by focusing on God and lost people. We want worship that truly honours God by accommodating those who are

---

[1] Joel Edwards, *IDEA* March/April 2003, p. 3.

[2] James Emery White, *Rethinking the Church* (Baker, 1997), pp. 80–81.

[3] Martin Wroe and Adrian Reith, *101 Things to Do with a Dull Church* (IVP, 1994).

seeking him. If as Christians the way we are together with God is a barrier to someone else getting together with God, then there is something wrong with the way we are together with God. It is a biblical principle to be sensitive towards outsiders.

Being sensitive towards outsiders doesn't always call for radical change. It doesn't necessarily mean changing the style of worship, but it does mean helping the outsider to understand it. Note there is a difference between being seeker-centred and seeker-sensitive. Being seeker-centred means having a service that is targeted solely at non-Christians – everything is done with outsiders in mind. Where a local church has this kind of service, there must be another opportunity for believers to worship. A seeker-sensitive service, on the other hand, is one where Christians meet together to worship God in an inclusive way, wanting their worship to be a witness that draws outsiders in.

Being seeker-sensitive

> can be as simple as providing Bibles for those who don't have them or offering a degree of anonymity for first-time guests who don't wish to have their visit brought to everyone's attention. Simply imagine what it would be like to attend a service without the background or knowledge to know how to participate. When to stand, when to sit, what to recite, how to respond – this is unknown territory to a seeker. Seeker sensitive has nothing to do with changing the church's message, just the church's manners.[4]

Worship for both Christians and non-Christians needs to be inspirational. One of the eight quality characteristics for a healthy church mentioned by Christian Schwarz in *Natural Church Development* is 'Inspiring Worship': 'While the question whether a church service targets primarily non-Christians has no apparent relationship to church growth, there is indeed a strong correlation between an "inspired worship

---

[4] James Emery White, *Rethinking the Church* (Baker, 1997), p. 86.

experience" and a church's quality and quantity.' Schwarz defines 'inspiring':

> to be understood in the literal sense of inspiratio and means an inspiredness which comes from the Spirit of God. Whenever the Holy Spirit is truly at work (and His presence is not merely presumed), He will have a concrete effect upon the way a worship service is conducted, including the atmosphere of a gathering. People attending truly 'inspired' services typically indicate that 'going to church is fun'.[5]

Worship is often a point of controversy when a church begins to reach the unchurched. It can be a painful time for both congregation and leaders. There are so many different styles and patterns of worship. Each church probably has a range of worship that fits within certain boundaries. On a scale of 1 to 100 (with 1 representing informal lively charismatic worship, and 100 representing very formal, highly liturgical worship), each church probably finds itself, say, in the scale of 20 to 40, or 60 to 80, or 10 to 30, or 50 to 70. Few, if any, churches will embrace the full range of worship styles. The boundaries are normally set by the majority of the congregation, with a few people at either end pushing in the direction they believe the church should move. Some want much more formal, traditional and quieter worship, and some want more informal and livelier, more contemporary worship. These are points of tension. A church may either extend its boundaries in both directions and embrace much more flexible styles of worship, or it may move both boundaries simultaneously up or down the scale.

Worship styles are determined by a variety of factors, such as denomination affiliation, tradition, age of church and age of congregation. Whichever style or pattern of worship a church

---

[5] Christian Schwarz, *Natural Church Development* (Church Smart Resources, 1996), p. 31.

incorporates, what is offered needs to follow the requirements given by Jesus: 'God is spirit, and his worshippers must worship in spirit and in truth' (John 4:24). Archbishop William Temple's well-known definition of worship is still one of the best: 'The submission of all our nature to God; the quickening of the conscience by his holiness; the nourishment of the mind with his truth; the purifying of the imagination by his beauty; the opening of the heart to his love; the surrender of the will to his purpose.'[6] Such worship will be a positive experience.

A positive experience of worship can be found among a whole range of styles. Broadly speaking, it is easy to identify several church categories:

- Traditional churches.
- Contemporary churches.
- Blended churches (a mix of traditional and contemporary).
- Seeker-sensitive churches.
- Seeker-centred churches.
- Multiple-track churches (offering more than one style of worship).

There is no one correct style, so many churches incorporate elements of more than one style. It is a mistake to think that only one type of church can be effective during the twenty-first century.

Whatever your preferred style, the prophet's experience in Isaiah 6:1–8 describes a pattern of worship that is worth following. It starts with Isaiah having an overwhelming sense of the presence of God. Every worship service needs to start with a clear reminder that we are in God's presence. The call to worship and the first songs can bring God's presence to mind. Having become aware of who God is, Isaiah then becomes aware of who he is: 'a man of unclean lips' (v.5). Praise and

---

[6] William Temple, *Preaching in St. John's Gospel* (Macmillan, 1939), p. 68.

adoration is therefore followed by confession. The confession is from the heart and is followed by the assurance of God's cleansing and forgiveness: 'your guilt is taken away and your sin atoned for' (v.7). Next comes the word: 'Then I heard the voice of the Lord saying, "Whom shall I send? And who will go for us?"' (v.8). Finally the response of obedience: 'Here am I. Send me' (v.8). It would be great if every member of the congregation was so inspired to action!

Give careful attention to linking together the various items of a worship service. I agree with Rick Warren when he says: 'Almost all churches need to pick up the pace of their services. Television has permanently shortened the attention span . . . most churches move at a snail's pace. There is a lot of 'dead time' between different elements. Work on minimizing transitional times. As soon as one element ends, another should begin.'[7] This is important in gaining the confidence of the unchurched, and also focuses believers on what they are there for. Untidy, unprepared worship does not glorify God. Prayerfully and carefully prepared worship enables the Holy Spirit to work through the leaders who have prepared for the service, and it does not rule out spontaneity.

Having said that, we do not need to fill every space. As long as we make it clear just what we are doing, we should feel free to punctuate the worship time with moments of silence, times of waiting, or open prayer.

I have become aware through my involvement in televised worship of how much time can be wasted. At Frinton there have been a number of occasions when we have broadcast our worship services live on national television and radio. On all of these occasions we have surprised ourselves at how many elements of worship can be included in under an hour. On Easter Sunday 1997 we broadcast our second service on the UK ITV network. The worship included eight hymns and songs, the

---

[7] Rick Warren *The Purpose Driven Church* (Zondervan, 1995), p. 255.

baptism by immersion of four people – each of whom told their story and were prayed for individually – a children's message, a children's song, a sung duet, three prayer times, a twelve-minute sermon and a closing prayer. All within 55 minutes and 40 seconds! That is not to say that worship services should be less than one hour, but it does illustrate how much time is usually wasted. More interestingly, and perhaps more significantly, the response of both the congregation in church and the viewers and listeners at home has been that the worship did not seem hurried. The many letters and telephone calls we received following our occasions 'on air' have taught us that commitment to excellence is a commitment that God can use powerfully.

If the church is to be healthy it must offer a quality of worship that fortifies the values of the believer and at the same time attracts, appeals to and relates to the unchurched. From the first days of the Christian church, both unbelievers and believers have been present in worship: 'So if the whole church comes together and . . . some unbelievers come in . . .' (1 Corinthians 14:23). But worship services have become the biggest barrier to the unchurched. This includes the whole worship experience: the physical environment, poor music (whether produced by an organ or a music group) and irrelevant sermons. It can all be a turn-off to both unchurched and regular worshippers. Boring, predictable and lifeless worship, along with sermons that are irrelevant to every day, is one of the reasons why many have either left the church or show little or no interest in attending.

Rick Warren says, 'Making a service comfortable for the unchurched doesn't mean changing your theology. It means changing the environment.'[8] The biblical principle is clear. Although worship is an activity of believers, it can be a positive and relevant witness to non-believers. How can we make sure this is the case?

---

[8] Rick Warren, *The Purpose Driven Church* (Zondervan, 1995), p. 244.

It will not necessarily be by changing the style of worship. The experience of many churches is that the quality, not the style, of worship makes it a positive experience for both believer and non-believer. Whether the style is traditional, contemporary or charismatic, a commitment to excellence changes worship from a negative to a positive experience.

The start of the service is important. 'If the trumpet does not sound a clear call, who will get ready for battle?' (1 Corinthians 14:8). Paul continues: 'Unless you speak intelligible words with your tongue, how will anyone know what you are saying? You will just be speaking into the air.' Have a clear, confident beginning to a positive worship experience. Too many church services start like a damp squib. The leader ambles into the service, and sometimes their voice is not clear, either because they have misjudged the strength of their voice, or the sound system has not been tested before the service. Some services begin with a catalogue of notices. If the worship service is to be a witness, let it express confidence, energy, enthusiasm and expectancy. Believers may be tolerant of poor quality worship, but unbelievers often expect more.

Answering the following questions should guide what happens in a worship service:

• What traditions of worship should be maintained, and why?
• What variations (e.g. interviews, changes in the order of service, video clips, people telling their stories) will be included?
• What's in it for the single mother, the teenager, the one who lost their job, the first-time visitor?
• What significant items can fill otherwise dead spots when people are approaching or leaving the platform?
• What congregational participation is appropriate in addition to singing and taking the offering?

- How should we improve the 'blips' (such as interminably long prayers and the public address system not working properly) that occurred in last week's service?
- How can we streamline some tedious moments (such as extended remarks when introducing items of worship, too many announcements and weather remarks)?
- What notice should we take of the Christian calendar?
- How should we provide for the varying musical tastes so that we achieve balance and quality?

Seeker sensitivity and cultural relevance do not mean theological compromise.

Worship includes the preached message and this is an area where the church needs to be particularly sensitive. Preaching a positive message is a passion of mine. There are too many negative sermons. People are hungry for good news. Mark tells us at the beginning of his gospel, 'Jesus went into Galilee, proclaiming the good news of God. "The time has come," he said. "The kingdom of God is near. Repent and believe the good news!"' (Mark 1:14–15).

John Chrysostom (AD 347–407) – known as 'golden mouth' – was a man regarded by many as one of the greatest preachers in the history of the church. He built his preaching on five principles:

1. An excellent knowledge of the Bible.
2. A good command of language.
3. A compassionate heart for people.
4. An ability to relate theology to everyday life.
5. A passionate enthusiasm when preaching.

These five principles are unpacked in my earlier book, *50 Ways to Help Your Church Grow* (Kingsway Publications, 2000).

Discipleship

A healthy, balanced church will have a commitment to people's spiritual growth. How do we help people to build a strong relationship with God? Whenever I have looked out over our congregation I have thought of all the potential there. It can be easy for a minister to assume that the majority of the membership are not interested in building a strong relationship with God. It is easy to assume, particularly in a larger church, that many people are not interested in anything beyond attending worship. It may be nearer the truth that more people are keen to develop their faith, but don't know how, or haven't even realised their own potential in Christ. God desires that each believer will grow in knowledge and experience, so the leadership of the church have a responsibility to lead people towards spiritual maturity.

However, spiritual growth and life change is a team event: 'Discipleship was never intended to be a solo event. Such things as accountability, ongoing challenge, encouragement and personal support are impossible apart from other people.'[9] Many pastors wish they had more time to spend with individual church members. New pastors just out of theological college often find themselves caught up in so many pastoral duties and preaching commitments that they ask the question, 'Just how do I go about building these people up in their relationship with God?' Sermons and Bible studies don't seem to achieve the goal. Some people know their Bibles from cover to cover and hardly ever miss a worship service, yet they still show little evidence of spiritual maturity. So what's the problem?

As Christian Schwarz reminds us: 'pure doctrine alone, as countless examples illustrate, does not induce growth'.[10] In

---

[9] James Emery White, *Rethinking the Church* (Baker, 1997), p. 62.
[10] Christian Schwarz, *Natural Church Development* (Church Smart Resources, 1996), p. 27.

other words, knowledge alone is not enough. Spiritual growth is not automatic. Many churches have acted as though either spiritual growth is automatic or their members simply do not want to grow. Apart from Bible study groups they make little or no provision to help members grow towards maturity.

Although Bible knowledge is vital, by itself it is not enough. Rick Warren says, 'It takes a variety of spiritual experiences with God to produce spiritual maturity.'[11] He suggests five questions we need to ask about whatever method we choose to help people to grow:

1. Are people learning the content and meaning of the Bible?
2. Are people seeing themselves, life and other people more clearly from God's perspective?
3. Are people's values becoming aligned with God's values?
4. Are people becoming more skilled in serving God?
5. Are people becoming more like Christ?

Typically, churches tell their members to become Christ-like, but don't tell them how. They tell them to have a daily devotional time with God, but they don't tell them how. They tell them to pray, but they don't tell them how. 'Effective discipleship will help people learn how to order their life around the attitudes, practices, disciplines, relationships and experiences of Christ. Once trained in this way, they are able to enter into training for themselves – training that will allow them to become increasingly like Christ.'[12]

People need to be helped, to be shown how, to be trained and equipped to be fully devoted followers of Jesus Christ. A crucial factor in this process is providing opportunities for relationships. People grow best in relationship with other people. Small groups are therefore essential to the discipling process.

[11] Rick Warren, *The Purpose Driven Church* (Zondervan, 1995), p. 340.
[12] James Emery White, *Rethinking the Church* (Baker Books, 1997), p. 64.

This is an ongoing process and a believer needs to be encouraged to join a small group on an indefinite basis. In such groups there can be a mentoring process, accountability, an opportunity for discussion and sharing.

Belonging to the family – fellowship

'Furious row over church plans' ran the headline in the local newspaper. 'A vicar this week offered up a prayer that plans to make his 100-year-old church more user-friendly would get the blessing of the parishioners.' Sadly, it was not to be the case – at least at first. 'We can't understand why the vicar wants to alter our beautiful church,' said parishioners. 'We cannot believe that someone new to our area thinks he knows better than local people who have lived here all their lives.'

Newspapers appear to love this kind of story. Is it because it fits the cynical image that many people have of church life? Parochial Church Councils, church meetings and elders' and deacons' board meetings have frequently been times of fierce argument. 'The church meeting was always considered to be the best fight in town,' said one man looking back on his youth, when he used to go to church. Division and discord are often present in the life of the local church. Broken relationships, malicious gossip and power struggles are not only tolerated in some churches, but actually expected to be the norm. The Bible meets this 'norm' head on: 'Make every effort to keep the unity of the Spirit through the bond of peace' (Ephesians 4:3). The reality is that there is an effort involved: 'Let us therefore make every effort to do what leads to peace and to mutual edification' (Romans 14:19). Unity and harmony between people, even Christians, is not an automatic process.

A sense of community is something to be modelled and taught by the leadership. If the leaders are united and understand the importance of being a community where people genuinely love and accept and serve one another, even though there are differences, the members of the church will catch the vision. Differences are not to be hidden, but recognised and respected. Real acceptance means looking at people with all their differences and accepting them for who they are and who God made them to be. A genuine environment of love and acceptance can be contagious – it can attract people to a church – and the leaders must be committed to this.

An important step in building genuine community is to build from the outside in. Make church membership matter. Offer a membership class that teaches what it means to belong to a biblically functioning community. James Emery White lists five things that usually form the basis for uniting a church:

1. Faith in Christ.
2. Values and beliefs.
3. Purpose and mission.
4. Strategy for achieving that purpose and mission.
5. Structure.[13]

He continues: 'If these five areas are not explained and protected through the membership process, there will be little hope for community.' A membership class explaining how the church operates is usually greatly valued by newcomers.

The way newcomers are welcomed and incorporated into the community of the local church is one of the most identifiable signs of health in a church. Leith Anderson says:

Healthy churches assimilate new people into the life and leadership of the congregation . . . One way to check the health of the assimilation process is to listen to how long it takes newcomers to switch their pronouns from your church and their church to our church and my church. Healthy churches incorporate new people as equal

---

[13] James Emery White, *Rethinking the Church* (Baker, 1997), p. 118.

members in a short enough period of time that those people do not become discouraged and go elsewhere.[14]

Ministry

It has been said that 90 per cent of the work of a church is done by 10 per cent of the members. No matter how hard you try, you'll never get everyone to commit to serving. Every minister's dream is to mobilise the congregation into action. The question is how to do it. 'Chances are that many God-gifted people in your church have not yet reached their potential. As a result, a ripened harvest awaits capable leaders who mobilise their lay people to "go and make disciples of all nations".'[15] Paul stressed that the task of church leaders is to equip people: 'It was [Christ] who gave some to be apostles, some to be prophets, some to be evangelists, and some to be pastors and teachers, to prepare God's people for works of service, so that the body of Christ may be built up' (Ephesians 4:11–12).

But turning members into ministers is a time-consuming task. Most leaders, particularly clergy, find themselves caught up in a multitude of other tasks. They are expected to be effective preachers and frequent visitors of people in the community, as well as in the church. They are expected to attend all the committee meetings, represent the church in denominational responsibilities, be a leader in the local community, meet with church leaders of other traditions, be good administrators, take part in school assemblies, speak at various functions, always be available, spend a lot of time in prayer and study, and discover the gifts and abilities of all the congregation! When regional church leaders, bishops, superintendents and

---

[14] Leith Anderson, *A Church for the 21st Century* (Bethany House Publishers, 1992), pp. 135, 137.

[15] Carl F. George with Warren Bird, *How to Break Growth Barriers* (Baker Book House, 1993), p. 163.

moderators ask a church what kind of minister or pastor they want, the answer is frequently, 'Someone who will identify the gifts of the membership.' In most churches this is far more than one leader can be expected to achieve without disappointing many of the expectations of the congregation and parish.

Thom Rainer, Dean of the Billy Graham School of Missions, Evangelism and Church Growth at the Southern Baptist Theological Seminary in Louisville, Kentucky, points out: 'The contribution of the Church Growth Movement to the unleashing of the laity is its constant, pragmatic questioning of "how?".' It is not enough to affirm the biblical principle of lay ministry; we must find ways of equipping people for their ministries.

Every church needs an intentional process by which to identify, mobilise and support the ministries of its members. Not only must we discover people's giftedness, we must find ways to help them use their gifts, and then support them in their ministries. These three stages – identify, mobilise and support – are vital if we are to unleash the ministry of church members. In too many churches the process stops at identification.

Preaching about gifts and every-member ministry is of course one of the primary ways of beginning this process of change. A long period of education helps members to rethink ministry, but they need not only to be taught and encouraged, but also to be shown *how* and *where* they can serve. In addition to the teaching and encouragement that comes from the pulpit and Bible study groups, more precise methods of preparing God's people are needed.

Over the years I have used a number of ways to help people know their gifting. I have never been entirely satisfied with any of them. We have tried some of the many questionnaires that are recommended by various para-church organisations, but none of them has been very effective in moving members into ministry. They seem to stop short at the 'discovery' stage. 'I've discovered my gift. Now what do I do with it?' is the plight of too many Christians.

As previously mentioned, encourage members to attend a course or group in your church that helps them to find their ministry. Be intentional about equipping church members for ministry. But what comes next is crucial, and we'll be looking at how we actually achieve this in the remaining chapters of this book.

Mission

It is God's will for his church to grow: 'All over the world this gospel is bearing fruit and growing, just as it has been doing among you since the day you heard it and understood God's grace in all its truth' (Colossians 1:6); '. . . the whole body, supported and held together by its ligaments and sinews, grows as God causes it to grow' (Colossians 2:19). Paul writes to Timothy, saying that God 'wants all [people] to be saved and to come to a knowledge of the truth' (1 Timothy 2:3). Numerical and spiritual growth is clearly God's purpose for his church, and this means not just increasing attendance on Sundays, but making disciples by incorporating them into the church family.

In Matthew 28:19–20 Jesus gives clear instructions to his disciples. He wants the people who become disciples, and are baptised and taught, to grow. In Acts 1:8 the vision is clarified and strengthened: 'But you will receive power when the Holy Spirit comes on you; and you will be my witnesses in Jerusalem, and in all Judea and Samaria, and to the ends of the earth.' In Acts 2:39, 2:41, 4:4 and 6:1 we see the outworking of that vision. In Acts 9:31 we read: 'Then the church throughout Judea, Galilee and Samaria enjoyed a time of peace. It was strengthened; and encouraged by the Holy Spirit, it grew in numbers, living in the fear of the Lord.' Here is growth on all fronts – spiritual and numerical; quality and quantity.

Charles Haddon Spurgeon, the famous pastor/evangelist of the late nineteenth century argues:

I am not among those who decry statistics, nor do I consider that they are productive of all manner of evil; for they do much good if they are accurate, and if men use them lawfully. It is a good thing for people to see the nakedness of the land through statistics of decrease, that they may be driven on their knees before the Lord to seek prosperity; and, on the other hand, it is by no means an evil thing for workers to be encouraged by having some account of results set before them. I should be very sorry if the practice of adding up, and deducting, and giving in the net result were to be abandoned, for it must be right to know our numerical condition. It has been noticed that those who object to the process are often brethren whose unsatisfactory reports should somewhat humiliate them: this is not always so, but it is suspiciously frequent. I heard of the report of a church, the other day, in which the minister, who was well known to have reduced his congregation to nothing, somewhat cleverly wrote, 'Our church is looking up.' When he was questioned with regard to this statement, he replied, 'Everybody knows that the church is on its back and it cannot do anything else but look up.' When churches are looking up in that way, their pastors generally say that statistics are very delusive things, and that they cannot tabulate the work of the Spirit and calculate the prosperity of the church by figures. The fact is, you can reckon very correctly if the figures are honest, and if all circumstances are taken into consideration: if there is no increase, you may calculate with considerable accuracy that there is not much being done; and if there is a clear decrease among a growing population you may reckon that the prayers of the people and the preaching of the minister are not of the most powerful kind.[16]

Healthy churches take the task of making disciples to heart. The Great Commission (Matthew 28:19–20) is important to

---

[16] C. H. Spurgeon's sermon 'The Soul Winner', as quoted by C. Peter Wagner, *Reporting Church Growth 1997*, pp. 17–18.

them. They plan a strategy of outreach into the community. They are concerned and pray hard when no one comes to faith in Christ, because they care deeply about those who are 'lost'. They are not content to be the 99. Disciple-making is exciting, thrilling, inspiring, challenging and transforming for those involved.

8

The Power of Small Groups

It is simply not true that as long as church members are committed enough they will grow and become effective disciples. Discipleship is not an automatic process. We need something more: 'And let us consider how we may spur one another on towards love and good deeds. Let us not give up meeting together, as some are in the habit of doing, but let us encourage one another – and all the more as you see the Day approaching' (Hebrews 10:24–25).

Small groups are an essential part of a healthy church. Build the same balance into each small group that is being built into the church as a whole. Whatever the size of the church, small groups are where God's purposes for the church can be applied and practised. They strengthen the whole of the church. As previously stated, it is in small groups that vision can be shared and owned. They will be a place of fellowship, belonging and pastoral care. Each group will be a place for worship. Share communion together if you are permitted to do so within the parameters set by your denomination. The small group is also a place for serving one another (ministry), and a place for teaching (discipleship). Make each group inclusive and not exclusive, welcoming new people (mission), and find purpose champions: a worship champion, ensuring that the group does worship together at appropriate times; a fellowship champion, ensuring that there are authentic connections; a discipleship champion, ensuring there is a systematic teaching schedule; a mission champion, bringing to the attention of the group matters of mission, both locally and worldwide; and a ministry champion, ensuring that serving one another is a feature of the group and the group might corporately serve in a ministry together. One small group in our church serve together in a soup run. 'Holistic small groups are the natural place for Christians to learn to serve others – both inside and outside the group – with their spiritual gifts.'[1]

Small groups provide a forum for deepening the church's purposes in individual lives as well as in the church. They provide a place where future leaders can be identified and trained – a leadership development factory. Groups provide a rich soil for spiritual growth and a safe place where sin and struggle can be acknowledged and addressed. Small groups promote community and life-sharing. It is in small groups that mentoring and spiritual partnering can take place.

Small groups are the pillars of church growth

Christian Schwarz says:

> If we were to identify any one principle as the 'most important', then without a doubt it would be the multiplication of small groups. In order to give proper weight to the strategic importance of small groups, we have conceptualised nearly all our church growth materials so that they can be used in small group contexts. We found that there is an enormous difference, for example, between church leadership discussing 'evangelism', 'loving relationships', or 'gift-orientated ministry' in its staff meetings and having each Christian, integrated into a small group, go through

---

[1] Christian Schwarz, *Natural Church Development* (Church Smart Resources, 1996), p. 32.

the process in which he or she experiences the meaning of these terms practically expressed in the life of the group.[2]

The structure of small groups

Churches with successful small groups tend to have strong leadership, organisation and accountability. Some churches follow the Jethro model. In Exodus 18:13–23, Moses' father-in-law helped him establish an organisation to meet the needs of the Israelites. Jethro organised each of the two million Israelites into groups of ten, with a leader placed over each group. A leader of 50 would then be over five group leaders. Next were leaders of 100, then finally leaders of 1,000.[3]

To enable every person to have a voice, a small group needs to have between 12 and 15 people. Finding leaders is not easy, but it is sometimes made easier if the responsibilities of leading the group are shared. For example, the person who hosts the group need not be the person who teaches the group. The role of teaching can be shared. Some churches are not prepared to take this risk, but future leaders have to be grown and they will make mistakes. All too often churches are looking for ready-made teachers and leaders rather than those who have the potential for leading and gifts that need to be developed through practice. Ask every group leader to identify a deputy leader who could be trained to lead a group. Again, use the group as a leadership factory.

Motivate members to belong to a small group

No church will ever succeed in getting everyone into a small group. In every church there will be those who resist joining a small group. But don't give up trying.

---

[2] Christian Schwarz, *Natural Church Development* (Church Smart Resources, 1996), pp. 32–33.

[3] Thom S. Rainer, *The Book of Church Growth* (Broadman, 1993), p. 295.

1. Communicate the value and benefits of belonging to a small group

One of the most immediate benefits that people may recognise is pastoral care, although sometimes this isn't realised until a time of personal crisis. Teach the value and benefits to newcomers and make it easy for them to get into a small group. A newcomers' group may be their first experience of a small group, and if the experience has been a positive one, they are far more likely to join a permanent group. But again, few churches are 100 per cent successful. Don't let that discourage you.

2. Frequently present new opportunities to join a group

At the beginning of a new term, after a summer or winter break, communicate the high value of group life from the pulpit and set apart one Sunday as a sign-up day. Make it easy for people to join. A good opportunity to join a group is at the commencement of a new study series. Group study and Sunday sermons can complement each other, providing another incentive to join.

3. Allow people short-term opportunities to try a group

This is one of the benefits of the short-term group such as a newcomers' group, an Alpha or other seeker group, and groups such as we had at Frinton: Maturity, Ministry, and Mission. Each class or group lasted approximately eight to twelve weeks.

One of the best opportunities we had to try a small group was a special period of 40 days called '40 Days of Purpose' (Lent may be a good time to try this). This was a spiritual emphasis for the whole church. It consisted of six Sunday messages, an individual daily devotional book by Rick Warren, *The Purpose Driven Life,* and small group study material. The Sunday messages were taken deeper in the small groups, and deeper still in the daily devotional book. At Frinton we encouraged people to join a small group 'just for 40 days'. We increased the number of our small groups by 50 per cent, going from 30 to 45 groups within weeks. We gave special help to newly appointed leaders. Some of them were nervous at first, but it was thrilling to watch them grow in confidence. The result of this effort was that many people who were normally resistant to small groups so enjoyed being in one that they wanted to continue. This is what Lyn, a newcomer to the church, had to say:

> The 40 Days of Purpose study has clarified issues that I have been trying to make sense of for as long as I can remember. It is as if, until now, I have been attempting to assemble a very intricate object without the maker's instruction manual. My small group provided a safe, caring and supportive environment for me to discuss my new-found knowledge. It has also provided a much valued friendship which we aim to continue after the designated six weeks.

Beryl, a mature Christian and church member, says:

> For some time God had been speaking to me to come out of the 'comfort' zone and dare to do something I had never done before. I am 63 years old but God has promised that we shall be able to bear fruit in old age (Psalm 92:14). So when I was asked if I would lead a small group during the 40 Days of Purpose I knew this was what God wanted me to do, and I took the plunge – stepped out of the boat to walk on the water. I had never led a group on my own before so it was a bit scary! I have been amazed at how God has given me the confidence over the past few weeks to see that I can do it, and now I am looking forward to continuing to lead the group after the Easter break. Thank you for your prayers!

4. Celebrate the stories

In old-fashioned terminology, encourage people to share their testimony of being in a small group. Congregations will be more motivated to join a small group when they hear the value and benefits from other members rather than clergy and leaders. If people can stand up and say how much they have enjoyed and benefited from belonging to a small group, particularly if they were resistant at first, this will have far more impact than anything church leaders can say.

Maurice Rowlandson, who for 26 years was head of the Billy Graham Evangelistic Association in the UK, says:

> A couple of weeks ago, one of our ministers said, 'We've already had a miracle. Maurice has joined a small group!' In doing so I am not alone. Others, who for various reasons have never been members of a small group, have also decided to make a special effort for six weeks. I have to say that I am motivated especially because I am the director of the 40 Days of Purpose spiritual emphasis in our church, and I feel that it is important to lead by setting an example. However, I have also seen the importance of bringing together three facets following the same theme: Sunday sermons, a daily devotional reading and further teaching within a small group. Only by sharing in a small group can I derive the fullest benefit from such an emphasis. I urge you to take the same step. If you've never been a member of a small group, put your prejudices aside, even if it's just for six weeks, and join a group. For the first time in my life I am now a member of an ongoing weekly small group in my church.

The Revd Norman Wright, ex-President of the Baptist Union of Great Britain, tells of his experience of small groups:

> I completed 50 years as a Baptist minister in July 2003. I have served churches in Northampton, Plymouth and Romford. I led a large 'Church Night' on Wednesday evenings in all three churches. Small groups didn't really enter our thinking. We were told that members preferred a trained person to lead Bible study, and often people said they were confused by all the different views of lay people who led small groups! Also there was the ever-present danger of a group becoming a clique.
>
> However, in retirement, I joined a small group at Frinton Free

Church, which has a membership of about 600 people. Immediately I was made welcome and played my part in the group, where I felt very much at home. The large church suddenly became very personal. I know that in reality nothing becomes significant or powerful until it becomes personal.

In our group we are able to share any problems, difficulties and successes. We are not a clique. The myth has been blown away! There is a real depth of pastoral care. Together we find ways of serving the whole church and, through the church, the local community. Our small group really makes the whole church relevant to daily life. After 48 years I finally joined a small group and realised what I had been missing.

These stories show that people can be motivated and persuaded to join a small group once they have understood the benefits. Normally, younger people have less difficulty getting involved in small groups. It is older people who are harder to persuade. These stories show that it can be done. For such long-standing Christians as these, it takes courage to stand up in front of a congregation and tell how they changed.

The 'what' and 'how' of small groups

It is important that small groups have a sense of purpose as well as a sense of belonging. Their function should be measurable, not just in the accumulation of Bible knowledge, but in the way they provide soil for spiritual growth, where community life can be shared, where 'next steps' are identified. People are more likely to join a group if they feel it is achieving something – if it is going somewhere.

Just as the whole church makes the transition to become balanced in its life and ministry, so the small groups need to be transitioned to achieve balance and become more than cliques or study groups.

The leaders need to form a network themselves so that every leader is supported, encouraged, trained and accountable.

They form their own small group in that whenever they meet together they can worship, have fellowship, serve one another, learn together and recognise the mission opportunities of small groups. There may be more than one leader in each group. The person who leads is not necessarily the one who does all the teaching. Those who teach may not necessarily be good at leadership. Leadership requires people skills, vision-building ability and a pastoral heart. Some churches view their overall leader of a small group as a volunteer pastor, who sees that the group is cared for and fed.

> Our research in growing and declining churches all over the world has shown that continuous multiplication of small groups is a universal church growth principle. Furthermore, it has also disclosed what life in these small groups should be like if they are to have a positive effect on both quality and numerical growth within a church. They must be *holistic* groups which go beyond just discussing Bible passages to applying their message to daily life. In these groups, members are able to bring up those issues and questions that are immediate personal concerns.[4]

Small groups have significant power for church health and growth, provided they are transitioned carefully and accountable to the church as a whole. One way of achieving this is to let the church leaders oversee the teaching syllabus and connect it with the worship services of the church. The groups have a life of their own, but they must view themselves as part of the larger whole.

Small groups need to be safe places for seekers and new Christians. Both need to feel free to ask their questions. If they're not, they will almost certainly leave the group and may never join another. There needs to be the same sensitivity

---

[4] Christian Schwarz, *Natural Church Development* (Church Smart Resources, 1996), p. 32.

towards new Christians and non-Christians as there is in the congregation on Sunday.

Some churches may need more than one teaching level in the small group structure. Obviously Christians need to develop their knowledge and understanding of the Bible and grow in their relationship with God and others. More mature Christians may be hungry for a deeper level of teaching that would go over the heads of new Christians or seekers. But it is not always the answer to put seekers in seeker groups like Alpha. Our experience is that such groups do not suit everybody, and there may be those who want to be in a group that is exploring issues of faith, but not necessarily the basics.

Small groups can be in different kinds of setting: in homes, workplaces, pubs, supermarkets, or even church buildings. Small groups are the key to pastoral care, learning, personal support and fellowship, but like the church as a whole, they benefit best when they have a sense of purpose.

9

Deepening the Purposes in the Lives of Members

Building a balance of biblical purposes into your church is a process that goes far deeper than simply changing the structure or developing seeker-sensitive services. Unless the end product is changed – and changing – lives, the effort is in vain.

Having discovered, as best you know how, God's purposes for your church, and having communicated and implemented your vision and restructured the church to serve its purpose, the task now is to deepen the purposes in the lives of the people. What you have done so far will have been a good start to the process. Watching people outside the church responding to God's love and care, and then making a commitment to Christ, is awesome. But something that needs to be seen by both existing and new Christians is that God has specific purposes for them as well as for the church.

It is so easy for both old and new Christians to think that it is enough just to have faith, or join the church or a small group. Most Christians are taught the importance of applying and sharing their faith to the world outside the church. They are not necessarily taught how. They are also taught the importance of growing up in their relationship with God, with other Christians and with the world as a whole. They are not necessarily taught how. The result is that many Christians have knowledge, but little application.

As Mark Greene has said, 'The Church, as the community of believers, is meant to play a crucial role in envisioning, equipping and supporting Christians for the life God intended, which includes sharing Christ's love with others.' He goes on to say:

> Research reveals that 47 per cent of church attendees say that the teaching they receive in their churches is irrelevant to their daily lives . . . church teaching is least helpful when it comes to where people spend most time – home and work. The Church in the UK has a 'convert and retain strategy'. Christ has a 'disciple and release' strategy. Are we making disciples?[1]

Beware of the myths that say spiritual growth is automatic, and once someone becomes a Christian, it is their own responsibility to follow through with a commitment to spiritual growth. Neither of these two views is correct. Spiritual growth and developing commitment happen not in isolation, but in community.

God has a purpose for each person in your church, and he has a purpose for each person outside of your church. Those purposes are discovered through a personal relationship with Christ and through belonging to his family, the church, the body of Christ. The apostle Paul makes it very clear that God has a purpose for each person in the church: 'Now to each one the manifestation of the Spirit is given for the common good' (1 Corinthians 12:7). The New Living Translation puts it this way, 'A spiritual gift is given to each of us as a means of helping the entire church.' That clearly implies a sense of purpose for each believer. And then the following verses describe what some of the gifts are. These are only examples. There are other lists in other parts of the Bible.

---

[1] Mark Greene, *IDEA* magazine, March/April 2003.

God's specific purposes will be found by believers who involve themselves in the biblical purposes of the church – worship, discipleship, fellowship, ministry and mission. Hebrews 10:25 says, 'Let us not give up meeting together, as some are in the habit of doing, but let us encourage one another.' Help church members to understand not only the purposes of their church, but also God's purposes for their own lives. 'Meeting together' and 'encouraging one another' can achieve both levels of understanding.

Each Christian can be encouraged to view their life like this: 'I am a follower of Jesus Christ. As such I belong in his family – the body of Christ – and I fellowship with other members of his family, believing that I can best grow as a disciple by relating to my brothers and sisters in Christ. I believe my discipleship and spiritual growth is a life-long journey. Because God the Holy Spirit has gifted me, I am serving in a ministry of the local church for the benefit of the whole church "as a means of helping the entire church" (1 Corinthians 12:7, NLT). God has also called me to be a witness for him wherever I go, to share his presence and his message of love, forgiveness and hope, so that others may join his family for time and eternity. All of this I do to offer my entire life to God as worship.'

This is called being a healthy, balanced Christian. This is fulfilling God's purpose for our lives. Within this, we will find his specific purpose. It will involve 'being' and 'doing'. It will involve our family, our workplace, our church and our community. God may call us to live out these overall purposes in another community, or even another part of the world. His specific purpose will be discovered as we engage in his purposes for every created person: to know him, to belong to his family, to grow more like him, to serve him through serving others, to share him with others, and to worship him in our whole life and corporately with other believers.

Help people in your church to see that belonging, growing,

serving, sharing and worshipping are all important. Rick Warren's book, *The Purpose Driven Life*, will be a great help to people in understanding God's purposes. Do everything you can to help the people in your church to live their lives on purpose.

Deepening the purposes means that when people come to the worship services in your church they will sense these purposes shaping the church and its worship. Build a spiritual momentum that helps people understand in every worship service that the church is on a journey with God and with people. You are wanting to grow as individuals and a congregation in your relationship with God and one another, with the community and the world. This sense of expectation, journey and purpose is quickly detected even by the visitor. This sense of journey, purpose and anticipation is a vital principle. It is biblical. For example, Paul writes to the Colossians:

> We always thank God, the Father of our Lord Jesus Christ, when we pray for you, because we have heard of your faith in Christ Jesus and of the love you have for all the saints – the faith and love that spring from the hope that is stored up for you in heaven and that you have already heard about in the word of truth, the gospel that has come to you. All over the world this gospel is bearing fruit and growing, just as it has been doing among you since the day you heard it and understood God's grace in all its truth. (Colossians 1:3–6)

Let this sense of purpose breathe through all of the worship services. Leith Anderson says:

> The external appearance of churches isn't everything, but it is a sign of health. Those superficial appearances of health include the upkeep of the church building, invitations to the unchurched by church members, excitement in the hallways before and after services, and the sense that this church is alive

and going somewhere. Just looking and listening goes a long way in concluding, 'This is a healthy church!'[2]

Avoid telling people what *should* happen in their lives. Instead motivate them by preaching what *could* happen if they lived for the purposes for which God created them.

Building purpose in people's lives doesn't stop when the worship service ends. Allow them to feel God at work in their ministry and mission. Help them to see that their ministry for the rest of the week not only serves others, but serves God and the church. Encourage them to see that what they are doing in their particular ministry is enabling the church to fulfil its overall purposes. They are part of a team.

Make it clear that the ultimate mission of the church is to reach 'lost' people for Jesus Christ, to make other disciples. When Dr Nigel Wright became President of the Baptist Union, he quoted Sir John Seeley, who said decades ago, 'When the power of reclaiming the lost dies out of the Church, the Church ceases to be the Church.' Nigel went on to say: 'It is surprising to me how many churches have yet to cotton on to the fact that unless we engage our communities in mission we don't stand a chance of surviving.' Mission is our overall purpose. The church needs to care about 'lost' people because that is who God cares about.

Encourage people to join a small group, for as already seen in an earlier chapter, this is where people will best grow. And each group will have opportunities for worship, fellowship, serving, reaching out and of course growing. God's purposes for individual lives are reinforced in the small groups. As already stated, deepening the purposes in the church from the worship services, through the weekly ministries and mission of the church, also means transitioning the small groups to reflect

---

[2] Leith Anderson, *A Church for the 21st Century* (Bethany House, 1992), p. 142.

those purposes. In small groups it is possible to mentor individual believers.

So how can local churches deepen the discipleship process throughout the lives of their members? If a local church has begun to build its life around the ministries and mission of the church described in Acts 2, then the same strategy of balance and health needs to be applied in the lives of individual church members. Help people to become fully devoted followers of Jesus Christ.

Church leaders are the facilitators of this process. As the Bible clearly says, only God can bring about the true growth:

> I planted the seed, Apollos watered it, but God made it grow. So neither he who plants nor he who waters is anything, but only God, who makes things grow. The man who plants and the man who waters have one purpose, and each will be rewarded according to his own labour. For we are God's fellow-workers; you are God's field, God's building. (1 Corinthians 3:6–9)

Only God can bring true growth, but leaders have a responsibility to prepare for growth. They expect and plan for growth. At the same time they look to God for growth.

Commenting on the parable of the growing seed in Mark 4:26–29, Christian Schwarz says,

> This parable clearly shows what people can and should do, and what they cannot do. They should sow and harvest. What they cannot do is this: they cannot bring forth the fruit. I understand this principle to be the very essence of church growth. Some do it deliberately, others by instinct. It doesn't really matter. Ultimately, what counts is applying this principle.[3]

---

[3] Christian Schwarz, *Natural Church Development* (Church Smart Resources, 1996), p. 12.

Leaders have the responsibility under God to 'prepare God's people for ministry' (Ephesians 4:12).

Jesus said in Mark 8:34, 'If anyone would come after me, he must deny himself and take up his cross and follow me.' And again in Luke 14:27, 'Anyone who does not carry his cross and follow me cannot be my disciple.' A definition of a disciple of Christ would include the following:

- A commitment to become like Christ.
- A commitment to prayer and regular systematic reading and studying of the Bible.
- A commitment to the body of Christ, the church.
- A commitment to serve in the church and the world.
- A commitment to share Christ with those who don't yet truly know him.

How do we help people begin to make these commitments?

Understand what people mean by commitment

The church often makes the mistake of starting where the church is rather than where the people are, both inside and outside the church. Look at people's existing commitments. For some it will be their career. For others, sport, the local pub, the family – all kinds of things. Then ask the question, 'What are they *not* committed to? Often the answer is 'long-term commitments'. The church affords a genuine opportunity for enjoyable, long-term commitment.

Give people a picture of commitment

Use biblical passages, faith stories, small group structures and worship services to encourage commitment to Christ. Give people models of commitment. People respond best when they see ordinary people who have made a spiritual journey. They sense when a church is alive and going somewhere.

Give people a place to make commitments

Small groups that teach the purposes of the church are places where people can make commitments. After a seeker group, such as an Alpha course, people can make an initial commitment to God. In a newcomers' or new members' group they can make a commitment to membership. They can make a commitment to grow in a discipleship group, a commitment to serve in a ministry group, and a commitment to evangelise in a mission group. Finish each group with a clear and specific way in which people can make a commitment. These small groups are valuable for providing people with what to do, why to do it and how to do it. For too long churches have assumed that people will automatically make commitments just because they have become Christians. Growth and change happen when personal conviction meets practical commitment.

There are five important principles in this deepening process:

1. Create a desire to move to the next step in the journey.
2. Show people exactly what to do next.
3. Give people a challenge from God.
4. Help people to grow one step at a time.
5. Recognise and celebrate each step.

Building the functions and purposes of the church into the hearts of the people builds healthy Christians as well as healthy churches.

10

Stories from Churches Building Balance

Some churches are already seeing the benefits of beginning to build in balance. The results are inspiring, encouraging and hopeful for the future of the church.

Here are twelve stories, each told by the leaders of these churches.

1. A Salvation Army perspective
by Major Peter Forrest

'It all started with a prayer meeting! The Leeds Central Corps of the Salvation Army commenced a prayer meeting that lasted seven days, and each day people prayed for the full 24 hours. An awareness was created that as a church we needed to seek God's will for our future. It was through this 24–7 prayer time that God spoke, and the Salvation Army at Leeds Central found its future ironically in its past.

'Let me explain. Prayers were being answered and there was great excitement and anticipation as to what God was going to do through us and in us as a church. At the same time a group of us attended a conference in Scotland, where we were introduced to the five purposes. While at that conference, as a group we were able to see just how we could begin to implement these principles in our life as a church. We needed to restructure the way we "did" church. Our organisation and structure was changed to reflect these purposes so that everything we tried was geared to reflecting the five purposes. So how did we find that in our past? The Salvation Army has for the last 20 years or so had a system of Mission Clusters as a model for organising church life. We saw the similarity, and with a few minor amendments that were necessary to cater for the uniqueness of our situation, we were able to implement a system that looked like this.

'We have five Mission Cluster Action Groups, each with a "champion" – someone who is totally passionate about their ministry. They have an assistant and the rest of the group is made up of church members who share that particular passion. The groups are Nurture (discipleship), Evangelism, Worship, Service to the Body (fellowship), and Service to the Community (ministry): N E W S S. Certainly good news for our church! Some of the successes are that the Nurture group has implemented a Newcomers' group as a first step in to fellowship, where newcomers can get to meet other newcomers and also the church officers. This has been so necessary with 40 newcomers this last year needing to be integrated and commence their own pilgrimage in faith. The Mission Clusters replace an Advisory Council that at its best could only number 17 people. Now because of the freestyle of membership of these groups there are over 60 people involved, all working in their own "passion field". We are presently achieving five times as much in the way of ministry. As a church of approximately 190 members, the implementation of the five purposes has given new life into a system that had been outgrown because of ministry potential.

'Continuity of purpose and accountability of mission are maintained by a co-ordinating council that meets every nine months. Here the big picture is painted and the vision is cast and then the Mission Clusters will take away to their respective groups that part to which they are most suited to work on. We have a mission statement that we believe was given by God to his people at Leeds Central, so everything we seek to do must result in furthering our stated mission. If it doesn't then we seriously think about not doing it!

'The result has been a new ownership by the people of their church and a freeing up of the pastors to fulfil their calling as shepherds of the flock and communicators of the gospel of Jesus Christ to a world in great need.'

2. A Baptist church in Essex
by the Revd John Davies

'The idea of building around five purposes was presented in the London Borough of Havering at a time when Hornchurch Baptist Church (HBC) was needing a focus for growth, direction and new inspiration. As the minister, I caught the heart for the key purposes of God presented in the seminars, and after prayer and discussion with the other leaders arranged for a day away to explore possibly implementing the purposes.

'Such enthusiasm was generated during the day that it was soon agreed to implement the key principles, but we planned to do so over a three-year period. Incorporating major teaching courses needed to be spaced out so as not to overwhelm the leadership and avoid course fatigue in the fellowship.

'An ongoing problem in the church was to encourage new attenders to become members. Being a Baptist church, we had a programme of visiting prospective members and upon a positive report at a church meeting, would then vote them into membership. There were misgivings about this procedure, especially when no other organisation receives new members in this way, and when it is cumbersome and for some intimidating. So we adopted the principle of covenant membership as detailed in the Purpose-Driven Church model. Now, when a non-member completes this course and agrees with our covenant statements, they are included into membership through the leadership.

'We are less than six months into the three-year implementation process, but we have already found real benefits. Out of a regular church attendance of about 100, 55 people attended a series of newcomers' courses, eleven of whom were non-members. Ten of them became members on completing the course.

'The key teaching package is the Ministry course, which enables each individual to assess how God has gifted and shaped them for service in the church and community. By the end of it, each participant has a one-to-one reflection to confirm the sort of service they should engage in. Although we have not yet completed the first Ministry course, those attending realise this is such an important issue. I certainly see this as a fundamental process for church growth.

'Perhaps the most important aspect of this balanced process is that it is seen as establishing a foundation for growth. We desire not just to see new Christians filling the empty seats in the church, but that they become mature Christians serving in ways that God has gifted them.

'We still have a long way to go to establish these foundations, but we are finding that real growth, direction and inspiration are achieved each step of the way.'

3. A rural church in Devon
by the Revd Richard Starling

'East Dartmoor Baptist Church (EDBC) was formed as rural congregations came together for mutual support and mission. A shared minister and preaching team gave consistent Bible teaching, and a joint budget proved helpful. Over time, we increased to five congregations, our smallest having a handful of attenders, and the largest over 100 on Sunday morning.

'By the mid-90s, EDBC needed new vision and fresh

purpose. This implied changes in the structure of the church. We launched a new vision statement, which was greeted enthusiastically, but having a slogan didn't change much. We needed renewed desire for worship and mission.

'As we developed our thinking, we encountered the Purpose-Driven Church model. Many things we had begun to discover were being taught in a coherent framework. The key emphasis was church health. We began to seek a balance between worship, fellowship, discipleship, mission and helping church members develop their gifting to serve.

'Chudleigh is an exciting story. In 1998, the congregation numbered about a dozen, but there was a desire present to see growth. Prayer gatherings began, and we dreamed of a new congregation effectively reaching the community. God guided us to relaunch Sunday worship with a new focus for the new millennium. In faith, we booked the local youth centre for Sunday mornings, and we planned services to meet the needs of seekers and the "fringe". With faith and patience, older members accepted change, sacrificing personal preferences for church growth. God honoured this, and within three years the youth centre became too small. We moved into the school for more space and a swimming-pool we use for baptisms. Growth from 12 to 80 is just the beginning.

'Numbers at Bovey Tracey have increased steadily, and the number of believers being baptised has increased dramatically. EDBC is becoming healthier through building in a balanced way. A healthy church is more likely to grow, in numbers and maturity.

'During Lent 2003, we held a 40 Days of Purpose campaign in all five congregations. This was very helpful in spreading the understanding of purpose more widely, and had a dramatic impact on several people. Attendance in home groups doubled, and we found the book *The Purpose Driven Life* both powerful and positive.

'EDBC faces challenges. Two congregations are in villages –

a difficult setting for mission. Our fifth congregation is small but growing. Perhaps home-based groups would be a more fruitful witness in a small community?

'Church growth is a complex matter. Because the Purpose-Driven Church (PDC) model is based on biblical principles, it applies to varied situations. Our application of PDC varies in each congregation. The common factor is balance between the five purposes, leading to a healthy church. This has shaped relationships as well as programmes. Because flexibility is built in – we are prepared to "experiment" with new approaches – congregations can see potential in their location, and try to respond appropriately. Rick Warren talks about seeing what God is doing, and catching the wave. This describes what we are trying to do in Devon.'

4. Hounslow Pentecostal Church, West London
by Pastor Mark Macklin

'"Balance is a word for wimps; extremism rules in every area of life." This attitude will almost always be reflected in how we respond in church life. We're hot on evangelism, worship or the latest revelation, but to the exclusion of everything else. These "shows" of fervour will no doubt be driven by a well-meaning leader or leadership team, leaving the people to wonder whether there is more to the church than the latest polarisation or, at worst, "What next?"

'When you begin to understand the concept of balancing the five purposes, as seen in Acts 2, extremism doesn't appear so attractive. Indeed here at Hounslow Pentecostal Church we have always been very strong in the area of worship and I really thank God for this heritage. But as we began to dig into the understanding of balance, we soon saw that we had areas of real weakness. Hot on worship, but not so hot on evangelism. Hot on fellowship, but not so hot on discipleship. In practice it follows that if we could ever get over the weakness in evangelism we would have people in the church who would enjoy a great worship experience but have limited choice in the area of discipleship.

'In seeking to address the situation I would stress that timing to recover balance is the key. If you picture any moving object that needs a course correction you will see that you cannot just grab the wheel and yell at the passengers to hold tight. As a church we have spent a long time praying and slowly bringing the change that we feel before God is right for us. God has a unique blueprint for every local church, and that blueprint must embrace the teaching of the early church.

'The idea of classes that give you the pegs on which to hang the five purposes is a great way to start. For us, building the first class (membership) and seeing it work so well was a great encouragement to continue pressing forward. People who were coming to partner us knew what was expected of them right from the start.

'The purposes need to be communicated both practically and from the platform. We need to teach people the importance of living the purposes out in the real world. The 40 Days of Purpose was a significant tool for our church as it earthed the purposes in real everyday experience. For many people this season was when things really fell into place and there was an enormous leap forward in understanding. The three or so years of preparation and foundation-building came to fruition in an exciting moment when we saw the church's spiritual temperature soar.

'We have decided to study each purpose for a year over the next five years, beginning with what we see as our weakest area. When we finish each year we want to see a strong team and a vision in place that will ensure that the purpose highlighted in that year will remain strong in every area of church operation.

'Developing and deepening the purposes in the life of a church is not another programme running for a limited period, but a radical transformation of our understanding of what should be central to creating a healthy church in the twenty-first century. For us here it is an exciting journey that will cause us to be effective in our purpose to reach this community and beyond with a message of hope for a world without hope or meaning.'

5. Jesmond Parish Church, Newcastle Upon Tyne
by the Revd Jonathan Redfearn

'The weekly attendance at Jesmond Parish Church is over 1,000 during term time. A biblical balance has been at the heart of our mission statement from its foundation in 1861. The aim then was the "maintenance and promulgation of sound, scriptural and evangelical truth in a large and populous town". That healthy balance of guarding the gospel and proclaiming it is still fundamental today.

'From the 1990s the vision of Jesmond Parish Church has been explicitly expressed as "Godly Living, Church Growth and Changing Britain". Making mature and fruitful disciples who will go out and turn the world upside down is a major aim. Verses 28 and 29 of Colossians 1 are life verses for the vicar, David Holloway, who has led the church for the past 30 years: "We proclaim [Christ], admonishing and teaching everyone with all wisdom, so that we may present everyone perfect [mature] in Christ. To this end I labour, struggling with all his energy, which so powerfully works in me."

'David understood the importance of building up every aspect of the church's life and witness from the very start: crèches, children and youth, national and international student work, home groups, world mission, etc., as well as the vital contribution of the Sunday services, which must aim to have quality music and preaching. A staff team leading and developing these areas has grown over the years, and now numbers 30. Along with this is an unshakeable conviction that God wants his church to grow and this involves prayer and planning. In addition, though seen as part of the whole, there is a strong commitment to be salt and light in the local community and in the nation. All this, under God, has led to health, growth and increased influence in the world.

'The church is always wanting to learn and improve. Since 2001 we have been learning much from the Purpose-Driven Church model. Rick Warren's teaching on authentic leadership should be heard by every church leader every year, along with J.C. Ryle's "Evangelical Leaders of the Eighteenth Century".

'The "intentional" approach to Christian ministry is so important to effective programmes that help the church live out God's purposes. We have found the "5 circles" (Community to Core), the "diamond" (Membership, Maturity, Ministry and Mission) and "SHAPE" (Spiritual gifts, Heart, Abilities, Personality, Experience) helpful in thinking through our evangelistic and discipleship strategy. Our international student ministry had already started operating on the basis of the five circles. The Globe Café, run in co-operation with other evangelical churches, draws a large crowd of international students, who are then invited to church, evangelistic Bible studies and then other regular small groups in the church. CLASS, or Christian Life and Service Seminars, has just begun at Jesmond Parish Church, with many finding CLASS 3 on "Discovering Your Shape for Ministry" particularly helpful. The "core" at JPC is well over 300, but many of those along with many others want to be serving in areas best suited to their God-given SHAPE rather than simply according to need.

'One effective programme based on the Bible and Rick's book *The Purpose Driven Life* that the congregation has greatly benefited from is 40 Days of Purpose. The spiritual temperature at JPC is high, and since 40 Days of Purpose an opportunity to acquire an additional building for the youth work to grow into was grasped very quickly. God is growing his people in faith, love and service. To him be the glory!'

6. Upminster Baptist Church, Essex
by the Revd Chris Hughes

'A number of years ago, we started to implement the principles of balance at Upminster Baptist Church. The vision was cast and teaching courses were prepared, but after an initial burst of enthusiasm, the vision lost its lustre. We became distracted and discouraged, and lost our focus.

'Then we regained our vision and momentum by using a spiritual growth emphasis called 40 Days of Purpose. Immediately we began to see the benefits of building around the five purposes of worship, fellowship, discipleship, ministry and mission. There was a higher level of commitment to worship and to small group life. We more than doubled the number of people attending our small groups. These groups are continuing.

'A buzz of expectancy and anticipation was felt around the church as people talked about the five purposes and began to see them impact their lives as they related them to daily life. There was a new sense of oneness and togetherness in the church. Everyone, including children, began working with the same issues and principles.

'The five purposes, or principles, were brought into sharper focus, with people seeing how they fitted together as part of the bigger picture of what the church was all about. This had not happened before. There was a greater willingness to take the next step in personal and corporate growth in response to the preaching. For some this was to attend an Alpha course; for others it meant attending the membership group; while others signed up for the maturity or discipleship group, and the two ministry courses that were arranged.

'For about 70 people, the next step was a new commitment to mission, by offering the *So Who is This Jesus?* video to about 1,000 homes in our surrounding community.'

7. Ayr Baptist Church
by the Revd Noel McCullins

'Ayr Baptist Church has a long evangelical heritage, ever since Charles Haddon Spurgeon recommended to the church a man who became its first pastor back in 1886. We have been a church strongly committed to outreach and mission, witnessed in the planting of a new church, the opening of a residential home for the elderly, and overseas missionaries in various parts of the world. In our own way we have been adhering to the five biblical purposes.

'During a sabbatical in 1991, I took a closer look at the mission of the church and produced a manual for our church called "Back to the Future". This was to challenge the leadership to look again at being the church in our generation. This started us looking seriously at every member having a particular ministry. Then in 1995 I read Rick Warren's book *The Purpose Driven Church* and immediately saw how it was possible to take what you already believed in, the five purposes, but rather than treating them separately, weave them into a meaningful vision for the whole church.

'We started implementing the vision gradually through various seminars with the leaders, and sharing the overall focus with the congregation in public services. Discipleship groups were set up to help people discover their personal giftedness, which eventually resulted in the leadership structure of the church being radically changed to involve elders and deacons as we applied the principle of gift-oriented ministry. The public worship services gradually changed as more people became involved in the music ministry and we tried hard to become more relevant in communicating God's word.

'In May 2001 I attended the leaders' conference at Saddleback Church in California and heard Rick Warren share how best to implement the five purposes in the whole church. This was to be another defining moment in my ministry, as we sought to lead the church into the twenty-first century. I started structuring my preaching to the purposes, commencing with a series on explaining the five purposes to the congregation, which was received with great warmth and enthusiasm. In addition to our ongoing discipleship classes we commenced our first newcomers' class with some new members, which I took myself and which proved a great success. Soon after that we added a discipleship class, with another teacher in charge.

'We completed a period of 40 Days of Purpose based on Rick Warren's book *The Purpose Driven Life*. Unquestionably this was the most significant spiritual experience we had witnessed in the church for years. We created 24 new small groups during this enriching and challenging time, many of them with non-believers in them, all excitedly studying the book. The Lord richly blessed his word during these six weeks as we saw people saved and others coming forward for baptism and church membership. Attendances increased and there was a heightened joy and expectancy in our worship services. We praise God for graciously revealing his purposes to us and look forward to what he has for us in the future.'

8. Stanmore Baptist Church
by the Revd Shaun Lambert

'When I first started at Stanmore, the church was driven largely by commendable activities and tradition due to a dramatic and successful past. It was mainly monocultural with little ethnic diversity, and nearly half the church was over the age of 65. However, I knew the people in the church had great potential. Seeking to transition to building balance through five biblical purposes has enabled a number of key things to happen.

'First, it provided something to unite the church. Second, it enabled barriers to growth to be removed. The key thing that needed to change was worship style, which was very traditional, and for Christians within that mindset, but was not accessible to outsiders and it devoiced younger Christians within the fellowship. The transition to the Purpose Driven Church model also brought me into contact with a network. One of the helpful tips from David Beer was to try and transition one purpose at a time.

'Worship was the key area that I was keen to be seeker-friendly and a witness. One of the first key steps in this was the appointment of a full-time minister with responsibility for music and worship – a purpose-driven appointment. Rather than just appoint an assistant minister who did all the things I did, we carried out the principle of appointing on purpose.

'Having looked at the demographics of the area and the church, it was clear that there were many people under the age of 35 whom we weren't reaching, and that Stanmore was multicultural. With Sunday morning having transitioned to a more contemporary and fused style, some of the barriers that had kept people away disappeared. Over the last five years, over half our new members have been under the age of 35. We have also begun to reflect the diverse cultural mix of Harrow, and have moved from being a very English church to one that has over 24 nationalities worshipping together. We believe the principle that the bigger skeleton the church has in terms of full-time workers, the larger the body can grow, and have invested in a full-time youth minister and part-time children's worker. The entire children's and youth programme has begun to build in a balanced way.

'I think the church in the UK has been reasonable at converting children and teenagers, but has failed to make them worshippers, part of the fellowship, disciples, and involved in ministry and evangelism. The five purposes applied to children and youth enable a balanced and healthy process of spiritual formation for them. Not only are they aligned in terms of purpose, but junior church teaches the same passage as adult church. As part of the way we are developing discipleship we also produce Bible study material for parents to work on with their children – both having looked at the same passage!

'We also produce weekly Bible study material for adults to work on as individuals and in small groups. Investing on purpose in people has enabled us to do that. We have invested heavily in technology, with all the services on PowerPoint, including the sermon. We have made our own baptismal and other videos of church life. We have seen the most conversions and baptisms for 20 years, as well as a 30 per cent increase in giving year on year for the last three years as people have caught the vision. We are seeing changed lives, with two young people at London Bible College and another three looking to go. Uniting behind the five purposes has enabled the church to negotiate many changes over the last five years, from a "solid" modern church, to a far more "liquid" but still biblically based church.'

9. St Helen's Parish Church, Trowell, Nottinghamshire
by the Revd Graham Booth

'St Helen's is an Anglican parish church in the village of Trowell, situated beside the M1 between Nottingham and Derby. It has recently become part of a United Benefice of three parishes, joining with Cossall and Awsworth. The population of Trowell is approximately 2,500 and the whole benefice 6,000, comprising very independent communities with different cultures and spiritualities.

'Over the past few years Sunday attendance at Trowell has doubled and we now worship in the village school, the parish hall or the local pub. This change was not easy. For many people the old church was very significant and they could not imagine ever worshipping anywhere else. Over the past two years we have become a "pilgrim people" whose identity is not dependent on where we worship – a people who have had to learn to worship in different buildings from one week to another and in new ways in order to reach new people.

'We have also doubled the number of small groups in the

church during this period. It has been very exciting to see the touch of God on many people's lives, deepening commitment to him, a growth in loving relationships and more people involved in a wide variety of ministries.

'Part of our pilgrimage since 1997 has been from maintenance to mission. This has involved us in looking at models of cell church, and through the insights of natural church development becoming more deeply convinced of the priority of focusing on balance and health. In 2000 we came across the Purpose Driven Church model and immediately warmed to its application of this principle, to its biblical basis and clear structure. The leadership visit to Saddleback, which followed shortly afterwards, was inspirational.

'Our church is very different in background and style from that of Saddleback. We are an open evangelical and charismatic Anglican church and believe that God has called us to be purpose-driven and Spirit-led – to balance purpose and presence. We are committed to seeking the guidance and enabling of the Holy Spirit and building loving relationships based on grace, but we believe that the best way to do this is one that is fully integrated with the biblical principles of a Purpose-Driven Church (PDC).

'PDC has helped us in many ways and made us much more conscious of the ethos of church on Sunday. Targeting particular services, we are now more seeker-sensitive in the morning. This service is also primarily aimed at young families. This requires a high value to be placed on work with children and young people. We have become more sensitive to what people will understand of the liturgy, of our informal "Christian speak", and of the words of songs and hymns. The musical style is still mixed, but is now more contemporary. We try to encourage the wide participation of children and adults in leading our worship, but doing things well is not always consistent with this and a balance has to be monitored. Generally we have invested in the presentation of the service, e.g. better quality amplification equipment, radio mikes, portable staging, induction loop system. We keep watch for wasted time and loss of focus at handovers, gaps between items, testimonies, repeated songs and individual items lasting too long.

'"Relevance" is a dirty word in some places, associated with compromise, but it is vital for us as we seek to communicate with our growing "fringe". Our preaching has changed dramatically over the last two years in use of language and in looking very practically at life issues from a biblical perspective. We have put a big emphasis on welcome. We want people to know that we are here for them. There are some specially gifted people in this area, but it is also a whole church responsibility. We use welcome cards, keep lists of visitors and issue invitations to regular informal welcome events. We have probably had more positive comments about this than any other area.

'We are continually developing a broad-based healing/ counselling/deliverance ministry to meet the needs of those who are coming to us. We know that so much of what we are doing is down to attitude: being willing to sacrifice – personally and corporately – some of the things we like for the sake of the lost. Our attitude has become "Whatever it takes".

'The emphasis on a balanced, healthy church through natural church development and PDC has helped us to think and plan strategically and we continue to move forward in many areas.

'Leading a church through major change requires vision and the ability to express that vision regularly and with clarity. We now unashamedly have an evening every month when we talk and pray about vision and strategy, and when necessary money, as the muscle of ministry and mission. Leaders are the key people with whom we share and achieve the vision. We are learning to invest more in leadership training and development, in-house and elsewhere. Key influences have been Willow Creek Leader Training Days and the videos and books of John Maxwell. Through this process of continuing change we grapple with vision statements and core values. These are emerging out of who we are, what we believe and what we are becoming. This is a slow process of repeated revisions, but is significant for the ownership of what we are doing and the quality of the end product.

'In Lent 2003 we did the Purpose Driven Life course – an integrated programme using the book by Rick Warren for individual daily readings, small group material (eleven groups at Trowell and one each at Awsworth and Cossall), and all Sunday sermons. The three levels together (personal, group and church) were very challenging, and helped both young Christians and older believers, particularly in personal discipleship and maturity.

'We are developing our small groups around the balanced life of the five purposes, though some of them also function in a particular area of passion and gifting, e.g. outreach action, music and worship, practical ministries, pastoral care, children and young people's ministry and creative arts. Other groups include Alpha follow-up, and groups that are more focused on supporting people whose primary ministry is in the world. We encourage members to be involved in community-wide special events, as well as giving personal invitations to barbecues and other non-threatening, church-based relationship-building events.

'We are aware that constant change is here to stay! Transitioning has become a way of life, a pilgrimage of process and progress, about risk, pain thresholds and timing. We try to avoid starting what we are not willing to see through and thank God for people of courage who are with us for the long haul.

'New things for the future include:

- a deeper level of engagement and partnership with others in our community through a "Parish Plan" process and accessing the Faithworks Network for help;
- building a new multipurpose worship and ministry centre;

- appointing a youth worker as our first paid employee;
- developing our witness in the surrounding area through the use of Willow Creek's Contagious Christian Course in our small groups.

'We couldn't go back now! We have experienced the privilege of God-given momentum and the joy in the eyes of those whose lives have been transformed, and this has whetted our appetite. However, we feel ourselves to be constantly struggling and juggling. At any one time at least a third of what we are doing seems precarious or even to be falling apart, but we are profoundly grateful to God for his work in us. We are also deeply grateful to Rick Warren and the people of Saddleback for modelling a servant heart so full of generosity. Their motto of "if this will help you, use it" has touched our lives again and again. So if any of this story helps you we bless God, and if we can encourage you more do not hesitate to get in touch.'

10. Shoeburyness and Thorpe Bay Baptist Church, Essex
by the Revd Jim Hamilton

'The key element of balance is to develop the purposes of the church in a structured way so that people are won for Christ, integrated into the membership of the church, encouraged to grow in discipleship, enabled to discover their ministry or service, inspired to be involved in mission, while all the time developing their love for God in worship that is creative and relevant to our culture and the seeker-sensitive.

'In the midst of all this we recognised that the church is placed in a geographical location, and God's purpose is to enable us to reach the people. To do this we needed to see that there are various layers, illustrated by concentric circles.

- First the *community* – what kind of people live there and who are we best able to target?

- Then the *crowd* – those who come occasionally to church. Do we have a means of knowing who these people are so that we can follow them up?
- Then the *congregation* – those who come reasonably regularly, but who are not yet members.
- Then the *committed* – the people who have become members, and accept this as their place of worship, however that is expressed.
- Then the *core* – those who are not only members, but who are involved in some areas of service.

'With that understanding the aim was to bring people through the various stages from the outside in.

'I had the privilege of going to a leaders' conference at Saddleback with one of our leaders, and the outcome was that I was commissioned by our leaders to have a sabbatical last year and produce an anglicised version of the four classes. The result was the "Shoebury Baptist Family Diamond":

- Entering the Family
- Growing in the Family
- Serving in the Family
- Extending the Family
- Worship at the core

'The Entering the Family course is for those who are interested in what it means to be a member of our church. We have run three of these now, as well as offering it as a day refresher course for those already in membership. Growing in the Family is conducted for the whole church – a fortnightly class comprising eight sessions followed by discussion in home groups.

'We then started the Serving in the Family course and so far 170 people have enrolled. It helps people discover where they should be serving and what they are gifted for. This was followed by the Extending the Family course. We wanted to run these courses for the whole church so that the concept could be owned, but in future they will be conducted in small groups on a regular basis as the needs arise.

'It is early days, but the indications are that there is a new lease of life about the church as people see the relevance of these purposes for their lives and for our church.

'Then last year we learned that Rick Warren had written another book, entitled *The Purpose Driven Life*, and it formed the basis for a campaign called "40 Days of Purpose". The British PDC movement encouraged churches to use the period of Lent to engage in this campaign. It basically involved four things:

- Sunday services based on implementing the five purposes in our individual lives, climaxing in special celebrations on Easter Sunday.
- Encouraging people to use the book as the basis for daily devotions, reading one chapter a day.
- Six special home groups devoted to discussing the issues raised in the services and the book.
- Encouraging people to memorise a verse of Scripture each week.

We found this to be a tremendous experience. More than 300 people bought the book and used it as suggested. It had the most amazing impact. Although we took the same theme at both morning and evening services, the attendances increased, especially in the evening. We involved more than 75 people in the various services, using dance, drama, music, flags and testimonies, as well as other creative ways to present the themes. We also produced a simplified family pack based on the book for parents to use with their children throughout the 40 days. Again this had a great impact. Our home groups were revitalised and increased in attendance, with special blessing being found in meeting weekly. Two new small groups were formed and will continue to meet as a new home group. There is a whole new buzz about the place as people have really applied the Purpose-Driven principles to their lives.

'I have looked at many ideas and campaigns over 30 years in ministry. So many have come and gone, but I believe there is something here that really can make a difference. The PDC principles are being applied in churches all over the world, with promising results, and things are gaining momentum. If your church experiences something of what ours has, you are in for an exciting journey. What could be more important than fulfilling God's purposes for our lives and churches?'

11. Balham Baptist Church, South London
by the Revd Steve Rouse

'Identifying the importance of balance has been the most significant change in our church over the last six years. Prior to this, if asked, we would have said that we did all five purposes of the church – sort of. We sort of discipled people. We sort of reached out. We understood worship to be what we did during the hours of our Sunday services. We spoke to each other after church and we had a couple of missionaries we supported. Understanding the importance of balance has caused us to become more intentional about attempting to carry out all the purposes equally well.

'We have found there to be three key benefits to balance. The first is focus. Having identified five main purposes for our church (fellowship, discipleship, service, evangelism and worship) we drew up a mission statement that encompassed these purposes. We have used this as a plumbline to measure the health of our various ministries as well as the church generally. This served to show us very quickly where our strengths and weaknesses were. The issues are raised and then we are accountable for leading the church to do something about addressing the imbalances that we see.

'The second benefit is intention. Working towards balance has made us more intentional in the way we do a number of things in the church. Its first impact was seen in the preaching programme. In each calendar year I would make sure that I preached a series on each of the purposes of the church. We also built in an annual Covenant Service, at which we would remind ourselves of our commitment to balance and then remake our commitment to one another before God.

'We also began to build in a teaching programme that sought to move people from a point of not knowing anything about Christianity to the point where they understand God's purpose for their lives and are living that out in reality. We based our programme on a bridge. We say that Christianity is a life-building process in which these five foundational blocks are built into our lives. This has had a great impact on our long-standing members. One lady who had been part of church life from childhood said, "I had always thought that once I got baptised and joined the church that was it – I didn't have to do anything else. I now realise that it's about a journey."

'Freedom is the third key benefit to balance. Aiming at balance has opened our eyes and minds to the possibility of each person making a significant contribution to the life of the church. No one person brings everything needed for the health of the church. We have begun to create a culture in which individuals are free to dream about church life, and some are actually seeing those dreams work out in reality. Recently we helped one of our single mums to start a ministry to other single parents. It's called The Well. She had an idea and we encouraged her to work it through, and now we have a new ministry that is going from strength to strength.

'For our church the significant benefit of balance has been the way in which it has caused us constantly to assess the health of our church. It is so easy to get distracted in church life and we need to be always watching for the imbalances and then addressing them.'

12. Christ Church, Belfast

'40 Days of Purpose does not mean 40 days of church meetings! Rather the focus is on three vital parts of the Christian life – the daily reading, the weekly sermon and the home group study. You need to buy the books and distribute them to everyone in the church, making it clear that this is a group commitment. These readings contain about 1,000 quotations from Scripture, which is an average of 25 verses of Scripture per day. Would you like everyone in your church to read 25 verses of Scripture every day for 40 days? What difference do you think it might make in their lives? The resources are excellent, with far more material and ideas than you can use, and a strong plea to localise the material to your own congregation and country. The Sunday sermons were given by our church elders, building on the teaching of the daily readings for the week, and providing points for further discussion in the home groups. At the end of the 40 days, you are encouraged to ask your church members what God has done in their lives during this period. These stories are precious, and even though you may never know all that God has done, what you do hear will confirm that God's word has made a difference. God has been glorified: what else do we need to hear?'

*   *   *

There are a growing number of churches around the UK and in other parts of the world that can tell similar stories. Churches that are prepared to learn from each other and network will benefit from each other's experience. Building balanced churches on purpose is one of the ways in which the Holy Spirit is working today.

Epilogue: The Results

A lot of churches are doing a lot of good things, but some of those churches lack vision and purpose. Sometimes there is no strategy. The many good things they are doing could be so much more effective if the creativity and energy behind them were harnessed. People are not nearly so well motivated if they do not know where they are going. Purpose energises people.

The churches that are most effective at reaching and keeping the unchurched are intentional about their purpose. Many churches do not have an intentional plan for reaching the people in their community. Intentionality includes practical things such as clean toilets, a well-run crèche, a welcoming environment, choice of music, sermon content, as well as the overall strategy of the church. Friendly welcomers at the entrance to the church can have an enormously positive effect. Well-designed banners and good lighting and sound system are all important.

Purpose and strategy can be the instruments God uses to spiritually reawaken a church. Rick Warren identifies four stages of renewal:

1. Personal renewal on the part of the leaders.
2. Congregational renewal when the church members warm

up spiritually. They want to be in good relationship with each other. They value unity as a priority.
3. Purpose renewal, when the whole church knows why it exists.
4. Structural renewal, when the church is structured around the purposes of worship, fellowship, discipleship, ministry and mission.

Rick makes the point that you do not start with structural renewal. Many churches have tried and failed. These changes must take place in the right order.

When spiritual awakening comes, four marvellous results occur:

1. Discipleship deepens.
2. Ministry multiplies.
3. The church evangelises with passion and enthusiasm, and new disciples are made.
4. Real growth takes place, spiritually and numerically.

God wants the people in your community to know him

That means you must employ the double principle of going out to where the people are and bringing them in, to build them up, equip them and send them out to bring others in.

Putting it bluntly, the people God wants serving in your church to make it a viable and effective biblical-based mission-minded community are out there in your local community. God has a purpose for them, just as he has a purpose for you. Hopefully you already know your purpose, but most of the people in your community don't. They are your future evangelists, but they don't yet know it. They are your children's workers, youth workers, church workers and leaders. If you want worker and leaders in your church, they are out there in the community. That's where you will find your future spiritually gifted women and men.

Our church needed another full-time pastor. Where did we find that person? Not in a Bible or theological college, or even in another church. True, he went on to theological college, but we found a top whisky salesman out there in the community whom God was going to call to full-time paid ministry! That was God's purpose for this whisky salesman, but he didn't know it at the time. Here is Ben Marlowe's story:

In 1993, having moved back to Frinton, my wife started taking our two oldest daughters to a midweek children's club at Frinton Free Church. They thoroughly enjoyed their time there and very quickly as a result started to go to Sunday school. I remember they used to come home from Sunday school saying, 'This church is so much fun, but if we go, why don't you go?' My wife said to me, 'Perhaps we should start attending Sunday services,' to which I said, 'Yes, perhaps we could go once a month, but you have to be terribly careful. You can so easily get sucked into these things.' As a result we did start to attend Sunday worship services and I remember thinking that this was the first time I'd heard that you could have a personal relationship with Jesus Christ. I thought that what we were hearing was either the biggest load of rubbish ever or it was probably the most important thing we could ever think about.

So began the roller-coaster ride of frantically listening, learning and searching. At the end of 1993 all that we had come to understand finally moved from our heads to our hearts and together we prayed to receive Jesus Christ as our Lord and Saviour. In the summer of 1994 we were baptised together – actually in the pool together – and I thought we had settled into a fairly comfortable pattern, happy with our new faith.

However, at the end of 1994, while attending a home Bible study group, I was impacted by Luke 9:62 'No-one who puts his hand to the plough and looks back is fit for service in the kingdom of God.' In the following week I found myself becoming increasingly restless. I sensed the presence of God, but there was no underlying peace, and in the end I decided to go and talk to David Beer, Senior Minister of Frinton Free Church. During our discussions David asked me whether I thought God was asking me to leave my job as a whisky salesman, which is what I was, and go into the ministry full time. I remember sending up a quick bullet prayer, 'Lord, what do I say?' And before I knew it the word 'yes' had popped out of my mouth!

So began a long process of testing the call to ministry, which resulted in my beginning a three-year course at Spurgeon's Theological College. This meant staying away from the family all week, only returning at weekends. I started that course believing I would leave college and go to another church, but once again God seemed to have other ideas and during my time there the leadership at Frinton believed it was right to test whether or not I was called to return to Frinton as Associate Minister. This was a call we felt was right and in June 2000 I was ordained, and inducted to the associate pastorate at Frinton Free Church.

Coming to Frinton as a minister was exciting and inspiring, but it was also very daunting because it meant I had to return to the community I had known and been a part of for so long before my Christian conversion. I couldn't help but wonder whether I could really have an effective Christian witness there, particularly in places like the golf club, where previously I spent so much time getting up to all sorts of things! In fact I needn't have worried. God of course was right. Returning to the community I knew so well has provided unique opportunities for ministry, and the fact that it was right was confirmed when the golf club voted to make me their honorary chaplain.

Ben's story is in one way fairly unusual. But in many ways it isn't. It is a story that has been repeated over and over again in many people's lives.

If you will take seriously the truth that God has a purpose for every person in your local community, and if you will offer yourself to God by saying, 'I'll do whatever it takes to reach those people,' he will give you the strategy that is right for your church. The principles and purposes outlined in this book are foundational to building great churches that will reach thousands. If you will implement them – if you will dream the dream – you could move out into your community with a Spirit-led strategy that will turn entire communities to Jesus Christ. As Mark Greene said:

> Imagine what might happen if we really believed in God's power to transform people's lives. Imagine what might happen if we looked around at the people we spend our days with and asked God: how do you want me to be good news to these people today? Imagine what might happen if we created Christian communities where people were safe to be who they are, and encouraged to become all that they can be. Imagine all this in a country where the overwhelming majority has rejected the Church, disregarded Christianity and doesn't even know why Easter is a public holiday.[1]

And, when you have imagined, step out in faith, using the principles we have looked at in this book – principles which are being tried and tested and enjoying the favour of God, who longs to see his church grow.

---

[1] Mark Greene, *IDEA* magazine, March/April 2003, p. 7.

Further Resources

A Church for the 21st Century by Leith Anderson, published by Bethany House Publishers, 1992

Changing World, Changing Church by Michael Moynagh, published by Monarch Books, 2001

Natural Church Development by Christian Schwarz, published by Church Smart Resources, 1996

Rethinking the Church by James Emery White, published by Baker Books, 1997

The Lost Message of Jesus by Steve Chalke, published by Zondervan/Harper Collins, 2004

The Purpose Driven Church by Rick Warren, published by Zondervan, 1995

The Purpose Driven Life by Rick Warren, published by Zondervan, 2002

Transitioning by Dan Southerland, published by Zondervan, 2000

www.pastors.com for Rick Warren's materials

www.PurposeDriven.com or pdcnetuk@aol.com for *'40 Days of Purpose'* and other *Purpose Driven Church* and *Transitioning* resources

50 Ways to Help Your Church Grow

by David Beer

There's a mountain of books on the mission of the church. There are books that diagnose the spiritual state of the nation. There are books on leadership styles, how to initiate change and how to manage it. There are conferences to motivate you, Bible weeks to renew your vision.

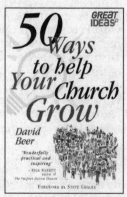

But it's Monday morning and you have people to visit and meetings to prepare. And there's a building to worry about, and junk mail to junk.

How do you tread the path between vision and reality? How do you get all that unrealised potential out of the pew and into the street? And how do you turn the tide from being a surviving church to a thriving church?

This is a book filled with hope! If put into practice, I believe it could bring about a mighty spiritual awakening that could touch every city and town and bring many to Christ.'

Rick Warren, *author of* The Purpose Driven Church

Communication that Connects

by David Beer

Most people in the Western world receive thousands of messages each week. How can we break in to share the message of the gospel?

How can we so organise our church life that we can get noticed in a busy, bustling world?

Having a message to proclaim may not be unique, but believing it is for everyone is definitely counter-cultural. This book will help leaders, preachers and those who share their faith to proclaim a no-compromise message in culturally relevant ways.

'Christian communication in its varied forms should have as its goal transformation and not merely information. David Beer expresses a clear commitment to this principle in a timely volume.'

Revd John S. Smith, UK Director, Evangelical Alliance

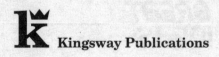

Kingsway Publications